CATCH 22

MY BATTLES, IN HOCKEY AND LIFE

RICK VAIVE

WITH **SCOTT MORRISON**

VINTAGE CANADA

VINTAGE CANADA EDITION, 2021

Published by Vintage Canada, a division of Penguin Random House Canada Limited,
Toronto, in 2021. Originally published in hardcover by Random House Canada, a
division of Penguin Random House Canada Limited, Toronto, in 2020. Distributed by
Penguin Random House Canada Limited, Toronto.

www.penguinrandomhouse.ca

LIBRARY AND ARCHIVES CANADA CATALOGUING IN PUBLICATION
Title: Catch 22 : my battles, in hockey and life / Rick Vaive and Scott Morrison.
Names: Vaive, Rick, 1959- author. | Morrison, Scott, 1958- author.
Identifiers: Canadiana 20200203487 | ISBN 9780735280311 (softcover)
Subjects: LCSH: Vaive, Rick, 1959- | LCSH: Hockey players—Canada—
Biography. | LCGFT: Autobiographies.
Classification: LCC GV848.5.V35 A3 2021 | DDC 796.962092—dc23

Cover design by Andrew Roberts
Image credits: (cover image) © Bruce Bennett, Getty Images

Unless otherwise indicated, interior photos come from
the personal collection of Rick and Joyce Vaive.

Printed in Canada

10 9 8 7 6 5 4 3 2 1

Penguin
Random House
VINTAGE CANADA

*To my grandmother Cynthia and my Uncle Frank,
who both gave me such incredible inspiration and
perspective growing up. Neither seemed ever to
have a bad day, despite all they had to deal with.*

*And to Joyce and the boys, Jeff and Justin,
for always being there for me.*

CONTENTS

FOREWORD

When I think of Rick Vaive, especially Rick Vaive the hockey player, there is one word that always comes to mind: *Why?*

Why, in the history of the Toronto Maple Leafs, is he so underappreciated?

Why is his number 22 not retired and hanging from the rafters?

It's a mystery to me, especially when you think about what he accomplished in his seven-plus seasons with the Leafs, and when you learn, as you will in this book, what he was dealing with in real life when he was doing all that.

At the age of twenty-two, when he admittedly wasn't ready for it, Rick was named captain of the Leafs, and he was incredibly proud and honoured to wear the "C." He became the first Leaf ever to score 50 goals in a season, and he did it three times in a row—54 (still the club record), 51 and 52. No one in Leafs history has done that. Over those three NHL seasons, only Wayne Gretzky and Mike Bossy scored more goals than Rick.

He played only 534 games in Toronto, which ranks thirty-second overall, and yet he still scored 299 goals, second all-time for the franchise in terms of goals per game. To this day, he is fifth all-time in goals with the Leafs, and tenth in points with 537. Everyone else in that top ten played anywhere from one hundred and fifty to six hundred more games than he did in Toronto. He had seven straight seasons in which he scored more than 30 goals. When the Leafs compiled their list of top 100 players all-time, Rick was number twenty. Of the nineteen players ahead of him, the only ones to not have their numbers honoured are Busher Jackson (sixteen) and Lanny McDonald (nineteen).

Then you think of when he was a Leaf: who owned the team, who was making the decisions, the coaches he had . . . I think what he achieved during that time is perhaps forgotten by some, but also wildly underestimated by too many. It almost seems as if a lot of people want to forget the 1980s because of Harold Ballard and the losing. Having said that, it's worth remembering that players such as Wendel Clark and Börje Salming were on many of those teams. They deserve all the accolades they have received. They were great players, great Leafs. But so, too, was Rick.

Since 1967, the only former Leafs captains to not have their numbers retired are Dion Phaneuf, who was captain for six years; Rob Ramage, who was captain for two years; and Rick.

I could make the case that Rick deserves consideration for the Hockey Hall of Fame, when you look at his overall numbers in a thirteen-year career: 788 points in 876 NHL games. There are other players, such as Cam Neely, who have deservedly been inducted despite having shorter careers and similar numbers. Another *why*.

Perhaps the fact that Rick had the "C" taken away because of a mistake he made (that cost him more than it should have) is a reason. But others have made mistakes, and at some point you have to forgive people and move on.

Full disclosure: I consider Rick a great friend. I met him in the summer of 1977, when I was working at the Orr-Walton Sports Camp in Orillia, Ontario. We had a training camp for the Canadian world junior team and I was the tournament coordinator. I went on to become his agent, first when he was in Birmingham, when I was working for Alan Eagleson, and then in Toronto when I opened my own agency.

I liked Rick's family. His parents, Claude and Mary, were typical Canadian Maritime parents. It was so important to them for Rick to do well. And he did.

Rick has never taken himself too seriously, but he was a competitor and hated to lose as much as any player I have ever known. He played with intensity and fire. He was a power forward and a great scorer. And he wore his heart on his sleeve.

In many ways, he never lost the kid within him. I admired that, to a degree, but it also cost him a lot.

In part, I suppose, because of the environment in which he grew up and the time when he played, Rick had a problem with drinking. He wasn't very good at it. And drinking cost him a lot of things: the captaincy, maybe having his number retired, maybe the Hall of Fame, maybe a good reputation. And maybe he would be remembered more fondly as a Leaf if he hadn't had the problem. Happily, it didn't cost him Joyce and his family. Joyce is an absolute rock. Ricky married very well.

To his credit, Rick tried twice to win his battle with drinking, and he has been sober now for more than eight years. Quietly, he has tried to help others in the hockey community who have had similar issues.

Rick should be very proud of what he's accomplished: from growing up in the environment he did—a small-town guy who didn't finish high school (hockey was his degree)—to making it to the NHL, to the 54 goals in Toronto, to being the captain of the Leafs with all the attendant pressures and responsibilities. On top of all that, Rick was dealing with undiagnosed anxiety issues, which no doubt made the drinking even more of an issue.

I knew about Rick and the drinking, but I respected who he was, that he didn't pretend to be an angel. And he was still a damn good player.

I also know that Rick has always been a good person. I know how much he loves Joyce and the boys. And I know that when he was captain of the Leafs, he always made the hospital visits; he helped people with disabilities, because he never forgot about an uncle who had an influence on his life.

Looking back, maybe there's a different question to be asked: Despite all that he achieved, what else could have or should have been?

I still prefer *Why?*

—*Bill Watters*

PROLOGUE

The irony was lost on me. I was young and having too much fun and, truth be told, I didn't fully comprehend what was really happening in my world. But years later, I got it.

Back in the spring of 1982, as a young captain of the Toronto Maple Leafs, I became the first 50-goal-scorer in franchise history. The night I did that, I came off the ice pretty excited. My teammates were congratulating me. The owner of the team, who was always at the rink and getting involved in team business, was nowhere to be found. There was no team celebration or acknowledgement. But I was given fifty giant steins of draught beer from a local restaurant and a "Texas mickey" three-foot-tall bottle of whisky.

The headline in one of the morning newspapers unwittingly said it all: "Me and the Boys and Our 50"—a takeoff on a popular beer ad.

Hockey and beer. They have forever been linked in my life. The irony? Well, that after the biggest moment in my hockey life, the reward was something that has been a constant in my lowest moments: booze.

My linemates that night—Bill Derlago and John Anderson— and I all had good careers, but we also had our battles with the bottle. In recent years, I lost a former teammate and coach in Dan Maloney to alcoholism, and a great friend and teammate in Greg Terrion, who I reached out to and tried to help. In 2009, another teammate, Walt Poddubny, also died after a battle with alcoholism. The list goes on.

Which brings us to the title of this book: *Catch 22*. I wore the number 22 for most of my career, and I became captain at age twenty-two. And it seemed there was always a catch to getting the things I'd dreamed of in my life, especially that "C." Damned if you do, damned if you don't.

When I was a kid growing up in Prince Edward Island, I was surrounded by drinking. I didn't want to be around my family because our house was always full of friends and relatives stopping by for a few too many. But I also missed out on a lot by not being around my parents and siblings. What's a kid to do? I wanted to be with my family, but being in our home made me want to get away. A Catch 22.

Hockey was my escape from that world, but it wasn't my escape from drinking. Back in the day, in the 1980s, drinking and hockey went hand in glove: after practices, after games, on the road. It's what you did. Some just did it better than others, and some more often.

A Catch 22 is a situation in which getting what you want spoils what you want. In my case, I wanted to be a good captain. And part of being a good captain means socializing with the team, bringing everyone together. But doing that meant I was swept up in the party life that, to a certain degree, undermined my career and my ability to be the disciplined player I needed to be as captain and a good teammate.

My entire career it seemed like I either couldn't do enough for people or I couldn't do worse. In Toronto, I scored 50-plus goals three times and 30-plus goals seven years in a row, but that wasn't good enough. I made a mistake, lost the captaincy and was eventually traded, and that hurts me to this day. I wanted to be in Toronto for the rest of my career and win a Cup there. It was the same in Chicago. I scored 43 goals my first year as a Blackhawk, but that wasn't good enough. They traded me, too. Then there was Buffalo, where everything derailed. I'm not blaming anyone; that's just the way things went. Shit happens. That also could have been the title of this book.

What makes me happy and proud, in the story I'm about to share, is what I was able to accomplish in my life, despite all I had to overcome. I have a wonderful wife, and we're blessed with two great sons, and now a grandson.

And I had a pretty damn good hockey career.

Could I have been better? We all could be better. On the ice or anywhere else. Some of my troubles I was born into, some I brought on myself. But I'm proud that I was able to recognize my problem and stopped drinking—once on my own and the most recent time with some help, but this time for good. And I mean that.

For many years, the ice—shooting pucks in practice, hanging out with the guys, playing games—was my happy place. It really was. But I am in another really good place now with my family, playing alumni games across the country, spreading a little goodwill through the game I once played at its highest levels.

I was with the Leafs from 1980 to 1987. It bothers me that this time has been described as part of the worst decade in team history. We had terrific players. My co-author, who covered those teams, once wrote, "The constants with the Leafs were losing, turmoil, and [Harold] Ballard, all of which might actually be redundant." That is so true. We had an owner who wouldn't hire strong staff, wouldn't pay the players well and wouldn't let anyone do their jobs. We weren't a well-run organization. And we all paid for it.

Another Catch 22: I loved being a Maple Leaf, but it hurt so much to lose and I ached to win. But I also didn't want to go to another team.

All things considered, I have had a good life. And I don't feel like my life is defined by my career. There were good days and, yes, there were some bad days, but it's like they say: what doesn't kill you only makes you stronger. And so it was with me.

I didn't win the Stanley Cup, but I eventually beat my demons.

This is my story.

1

PARTY CENTRAL

"I love you."

It's a hat trick of words I didn't hear a lot growing up, certainly not at home.

I don't recall either of my parents, Claude and Mary-Evelyn, ever telling me that they loved me. I'm not sure I ever said it to them. I probably did when I was younger, but as a kid you're not really thinking about it; you're living in the moment. It's kind of strange, really, how something like that sticks in your head. Was it the times? Maybe their parents never told them either, although I know my mother would have heard those words from my grand-mother. With ten kids in my father's family and six in my mother's, maybe there just wasn't time for sentimentality.

As a family, we never had conversations about how we were doing: how's school, how's this, how's that? But my parents did go out of their way to make sure their kids—me; my sister, Barbara, who is fourteen months older than me; and my brothers Steve, two years younger, and Ron, five years younger—got what we needed. They went without so we would have nice clothes to wear to school. We weren't the best-dressed kids in the place, but we dressed well; they made sure of that. And we had all the hockey equipment we needed, baseball gear, anything we needed for other sports.

I was born in Ottawa on May 14, 1959, and lived there until I was eight and a half. We moved a couple of times, but I don't remember a lot about those early years, other than that my dad used to make a rink in the backyard. We lived in a fourplex, a row of townhouses. I don't know if he coordinated things with the other fathers or talked them into helping, but he used all the backyards to make one big rink with lights—they used pie plates to make sure the lights would shine down on the ice—and boards and everything. I have no idea how Dad did it. He was a steelworker for the Dominion Bridge Company at the time, travelling a lot, but he'd still be out there at one o'clock in the morning watering the rink to make sure it would be good for us the next day. Then he'd get up and go to work.

My dad played hockey up to maybe junior B. I don't know if he was a good player—he never talked about it. He never talked about himself at all. I know only that he was in the middle of nine other kids and his father wasn't around when he was growing up; he'd passed away. He had lots of relatives in Gatineau, Quebec, and around the Ottawa area: brothers and sisters and their spouses and children. And he really wanted us to have the opportunity to play hockey. I don't think he expected us to one day play in the NHL or anything. He just wanted us to enjoy that backyard. And we did.

I was probably three years old when I first stepped on that rink. I didn't start playing organized hockey until I was six. But for three years, I was always outside skating, having fun, and all the kids in the neighbourhood would join in. I guess that's when my passion for the game was born. It was hockey all the time when I was growing up. And Saturday nights, of course, we'd watch the Leafs or Canadiens on TV. Dad would let me watch a period or two and then tell me to go to bed. I'd sneak down and he'd yell, "Get the hell back to bed." He didn't see me, but he knew I was there. When it got to the Stanley Cup final, he would let us watch the whole game.

My sister and her friends wanted the backyard ice to figure skate, so we had to have a schedule, which didn't go over well with us guys. We wanted our ice time!

That went on until my dad's accident.

I was probably six, maybe six and a half, when it happened. His crew was bringing a steel beam across a construction site, and it somehow hit him on the head and knocked him out. He slipped through his safety belt and fell maybe forty feet to the ground. Looking back on it, I'm not even sure how he survived. He was in the hospital for quite some time and had I don't know how many surgeries on his hips and heels, on everything that was damaged. He came home in a wheelchair and they thought he might never walk again. There wasn't a day he wasn't in pain.

After the accident, my dad obviously couldn't work in construction anymore. He was twenty-five with a very young family. He was a smart man, well read, so he started working for a company that made altimeters and instruments for aircraft. The bosses knew my mother was from Prince Edward Island, and when they were about to open a plant in Amherst, Nova Scotia, they asked my dad if he would go and run it.

When we got to Amherst, a town of about ninety-five hundred people, we didn't know anybody. I joined the local minor hockey league and tried out for the Peewee Macs. The team was sponsored by Mack trucks, and it was definitely the team to be on, because they travelled all over the place. But the kids on that team were eleven and twelve years old. I was going to be nine in May, but one kid's father said I might as well try out. I asked my dad and he said it was okay. I made the team. Even at nine years old, I was probably one of the top six forwards.

One of the places our peewee team got to go was the famous Quebec International Pee-Wee Tournament. The tournament is huge now, having grown over the years to include a few thousand players from a dozen or so countries. But even back then it was a big deal. We made it two years in a row, 1970 and '71, when I was ten and eleven years old. Both times we lost our first game in overtime (it's a one-game elimination), but we played a couple of exhibition games, practised on outdoor rinks and had the experience of playing in the Colisée, which at the time had a capacity of about ten thousand fans. Later, the venue would add more seats, and it eventually became the home of the Quebec Nordiques. I got to play there when I joined the World Hockey Association (WHA), and when the Nordiques moved to the NHL. As big as that arena was, it was often full for the peewee tournament.

Tournaments like that were an amazing experience, especially at that age. What was tough for me, though, were the nights away.

When I was a kid, I wet the bed. My mother was always having to wash the sheets and I would get heck for it. But I didn't know what the hell was happening. She took me to what seemed like a million doctors to find out what the problem was. They said take him off milk, take him off this, don't let him drink that—a million different things, and nothing helped. During weekend tournaments, I'd go two, sometimes three nights, basically staying awake. I'd maybe catch an hour or two of sleep. As a kid you need your sleep, but I wasn't getting it. I did that all through minor hockey. My whole life, it's been like this. When I have to go to the bathroom, I have to get there quick.

Hockey itself was going very well. I played in Amherst for three years, but then they shut down my father's plant. That's when we moved to Prince Edward Island. I was almost eleven at the time.

Life changed for the family, and not for the better.

When we got to Charlottetown, my dad started a painting business and my mom handled the account books. Our house was party central. People would just drop in, sit down, have a meal, have some drinks. Every weekend all of my mom's relatives would come over. They might bring a hamburger and a six-pack, but they'd end up eating a steak and drinking a dozen beers. They would all get polluted and then the arguments would start. I didn't want to be around it.

I used to go to my grandmother's house (my mother's mom), where it was quiet, unless my grandfather, who was an alcoholic, was on a bender. He would be sober for a while and then fall off the wagon. And when he did, he'd come home, yell and scream, and then pass out. Then he'd get up and go out to the bootlegger's, come back a few hours later and do it all over again. Sometimes my grandmother would call the cops to haul him away to dry out. But there were also stretches when he didn't have a drink for as long as two years. Those were the times when everything was okay, when my grandparents' house was a quiet place, a nice place to get away from the craziness at home.

It wasn't until later in life that I came to realize what a terrible influence all the drinking and fighting—at my parents' house, with my grandfather—had on me. Back then I was too focused on school and sports to notice, too focused on just trying to get through my childhood.

Thankfully, I had some company. My Uncle Frank had cerebral palsy as a baby and it left him disabled. He couldn't walk. He was blind and in a wheelchair. He lived with my grandmother. Uncle Frank loved music. He had hundreds of records and knew every song. My grandparents bought him a record player. He had a sixth sense of sorts. He would feel the grooves on the record and put down the needle on the player and he would know what the song would be. It was amazing. But because of his disability, while he could play records on his own he would often scratch them. So, when I would go visit and he lay down for his naps, I'd sit in his chair and play music for him—we all did that—and we'd hang out for hours. After I turned pro, for three years I had a celebrity golf tournament in PEI—Wayne Gretzky came one year—to raise money for cerebral palsy. Uncle Frank was the youngest of six kids in my mother's family, and my grandmother was always so patient and kind with him. Cynthia White—my grandmother—was a great person. She never had a bad day, or at least she never let you know it if she did. Even then I marvelled at how she could get through everything she had to deal with but still always be so upbeat. And she had to deal with a lot. There was her husband and his drinking, for starters. And then there was my Uncle Kevin's accident.

My mother was the first-born. Next came two more girls—my aunts Teresa and Barb—and then three boys: Kevin, John and Frank. While at Dalhousie, Kevin was probably one of the top players in Canadian college basketball. But he died in his second year, just nineteen years old. I remember my mom getting the phone call—we were still in Ottawa at the time—and hearing the scream. He was killed along with three other teenagers in a car accident near Peggy's Cove. They had been out partying after exams and were due to come home the next day, December 12, 1967. It was quite a blow to the family. So my grandmother had to deal with that, too, while caring for Uncle Frank 24/7. But even with all of that, she always seemed happy. She went to church almost every day, even for just an hour, and that probably helped her. Maybe her faith kept her going. She never really talked about it.

Whatever it was, I loved being around her. I always found the time at her house very calming. I think she and the example she set helped me deal with the chaos happening around me. She helped me to not get down about things, to try to stay positive, like she did. It worked for a while, but then she passed away and a lot of things changed for me. It happened in 1991, when I was playing in Buffalo. I went home for the funeral, but I didn't deal with it well.

It was very, very difficult. She was my grandmother, but she was also my friend, and I missed having her to talk to. I'd spent as much time with her as I had with my parents. She was my role model. When I looked at her, I thought, *This is how I want to be.*

And she told me she loved me all the time.

Later in my life, I didn't deal with my troubles nearly as well as she'd handled hers. When bad things happened—like her passing—I'd start drinking a little bit more. Drinking was the go-to, although it wasn't something I did every day. I wasn't a good drinker, that's for darn sure. If I could have a couple of drinks and then leave, I would be okay. But once I got to four or five, that was it; I might be drinking for five or six hours. I was able to live up to her example for a little while, but I had my parents' example too, especially at the end of my career, when I wasn't playing very much. But more about that later.

My grandmother was a hero to me when I was growing up, that's for sure. I really didn't have any hockey heroes back then. The only guy I looked up to, because he was such a great player, was Jean Béliveau, the late Montreal Canadiens star. On TV, all we got were Montreal and Toronto games, but I never picked a favourite. I didn't like Montreal, because my dad liked them. If he liked Montreal then I wasn't going to. Maybe it's just a kid thing, to go against your parents in some way. It wasn't that he treated me horribly—as I said, he did all he could for us kids—but for some reason I got blamed for nearly everything that happened around the house. It didn't matter if one of my brothers was actually the one who had done whatever we were getting called out on. I got the belt, or got grounded or punished. I certainly wasn't always an angel, but I took much more than my share of the blame back then.

I was the oldest of the boys, and my sister, being the only girl, was untouchable. That was fine with me; I didn't expect her to get the belt. So eventually I just accepted it. *They're my younger brothers*, I figured. *What the hell, I'll take a few whacks on the ass.* It didn't kill me. It hurt a little bit, but they were my little brothers. So be it. Sometimes I got angry at them for getting me in trouble, but mostly I just took my lumps and moved on.

Even with the unfair doling out of punishment, my relationship with my siblings was okay. My sister and I got along fine. It was the same with my brothers. Steve was a shit disturber. He was the guy always pulling off the pranks, always trying to tease the rest of us. He'd get under the skin of my youngest brother, Ron, and Ron would whine to Mom and Dad and my brother might get heck. But sometimes it would land on me anyway because Steve would say I didn't do anything to stop it, and then my parents would figure it must have been my fault somehow.

Back when I was growing up, the worst words anyone could hear from their mother were "Wait until your father gets home." One time—I don't remember what actually happened, but I was probably five or six years old at the time—my dad came home from work and my mom told him all about whatever we'd done. He grabbed me and carried me upstairs into the bedroom and threw me against the wall. I came down on the bed, and as I lay there, he said, "And don't leave this room." I'm thinking, *Yeah, sure. You just threw me against the wall. I'm not going anywhere.* I think that was the worst punishment I ever experienced. Not that it hurt, really, but you're five or six years old, so you're wondering what the hell this is all about. If something like that happened today, it would be frowned upon pretty harshly.

When we were really young, we would all sneak down to the Ottawa River in the summer and swing on a tire over the water. We'd be having a great time and then, of course, Mom and Dad would show up in the car and that was the end of that. We weren't supposed to be there. That happened three or four times a week. We'd get caught down at the river and there were consequences, usually the strap and grounding. I just kept going to the river until finally they literally tied me to the porch with a harness.

As close as I was to my grandmother, I never talked to her about my father or about anything else that was going on at home. I didn't want her to know some of the stuff my parents were doing. I figured she had enough on her plate, so I kept it to myself. I never talked about it with anybody. I didn't want people thinking negatively about my parents.

I've thought about it a lot over the years—was my dad abusive or was that just the way things were at the time? I always chalked up his behaviour to how he was raised, and to the fact that he probably didn't know any different. He was very strict. He used to cut all three boys' hair. We had brush cuts and I hated it. Kids would pick on me for having short hair. It was grade eight before I was allowed to grow it out a bit. My mom and dad were parenting the way they had been shown how to parent. But Dad did have a very short fuse and a bad temper. It wasn't fun.

Of course, I kept on with hockey in PEI. We may have had one of the best peewee teams in the country. We couldn't raise enough money to go to the Quebec peewee tournament, so we played in a tournament in Saint John, New Brunswick, at Christmas instead. A team from Pointe-Claire, Quebec, was there. They'd won the B division at Quebec, the division we would have been in, and we beat them 7–1. That was frustrating, knowing we could have won our division at Quebec but couldn't afford to go.

My parents created the Spud Tournament, which was a big minor hockey event for all levels. Teams came from across the Maritimes, and some from even farther away. My parents arranged the billets and ran the snack bar. My brothers both played in it. Our parents did a lot for hockey in PEI.

Every weekend we would play at home for two games or go on the road for two. My dad went to most of my games, my mom sometimes. Dad helped coach a few of my teams. But often, especially when we went off the island, I would travel with another family because my parents would either stay home or go on the road with my brothers. I understood my brothers were younger and needed Mom and Dad to be with them. In some ways, I kind of enjoyed getting away from home. My dad hardly said a word about hockey unless I asked him. He was never one to say "You should have done this" or "You should have done that." But if I asked, he usually gave me negative feedback. I stopped asking. I didn't want to hear it.

It was around this time that I started thinking in a way that would stay with me for my entire career. I figured that as long as my coach was happy with how I was playing, and as long as I was happy, that was all that mattered. I didn't care what my father thought. I didn't care what the press said, or anybody else. It was how my coach, my teammates and I felt—that was all that mattered.

Even though I didn't have a favourite NHL team, I did have a really cool experience with the Canadiens. In the fall of 1971, Montreal came to Charlottetown to play an exhibition game against their farm team, the Nova Scotia Voyageurs. Dad had converted my mother and aunt into Habs fans, but he didn't have enough money for all of us to go the game. He bought tickets for himself and my mom, and my aunt bought her own. I ended up skipping school that day so I could hang around the rink, waiting for the Canadiens to arrive for their morning skate.

Finally, Eddy Palchak, the Canadiens' long-time equipment manager, arrived with the gear in a van. Four of us local kids helped him unload everything, and he told us to come back around 4:30 or five o'clock. So we did. He sent two of the four of us to the Voyageurs' dressing room, and he told me and a buddy to stay around the Canadiens' room. So, here I am, a twelve-year-old, walking into the Montreal Canadiens' dressing room and handing out socks and tape to the likes of Henri Richard, Guy Lafleur, Yvon Cournoyer, Réjean Houle, Claude Larose, Jacques Lemaire, Frank and Peter Mahovlich, Terry Harper, Jacques Laperrière, Guy Lapointe and Serge Savard. I'm thinking, *Wow, this is pretty cool.* Ken Dryden and Rogie Vachon were the goalies. (I'd see Vachon again in a few years, when I was a Canuck and he was with the Detroit Red Wings.)

So, Eddy hands me a Canadiens track top and says, "I want you to take the sticks over to the bench." So I'm walking across the ice when I hear a woman—the rink only held two thousand or so people—saying, "That looks like Rick." Then I hear another woman saying, "It is, it is!" And then they start screaming. It was my mother and my aunt. I got off easy, despite skipping school. They were happy for me, that I got to do that.

When I was sixteen, in Charlottetown, I played for the Colonel Gray Colonels, a junior team in the tier-2 league. I also attended Colonel Gray High School, and one year we put a team together to play in a big tournament in Cape Breton, with one high-school team from each province. We won it. I think it was Upper Canada College from Toronto that we beat in the final. I was named the most valuable player in the tournament. Whatever was happening off the ice, everything was great on it. My teams won the Maritime championship my last year of peewee, bantam, midget and junior.

Off the ice, though, life could be rough in a small town. One night during grade eleven, there was a party in Keppoch, a cottage area over the bridge from Charlottetown. It was near the end of the school year and everyone was going. Four guys who played on the high-school football team, who I knew pretty well—we hung out a lot—asked me if I wanted to drive with them, but I had a test and it was my birthday, so I didn't go. Of course there was a lot of booze, like any high-school party. They got into a car accident on the way home. I don't know how much they were drinking, but they drove off the road into a culvert. The car flew up in the air; you could see a mark on the lamppost where the car hit it.

Out of the four of them, only the driver survived. We were supposed to have a party that night to celebrate my birthday, but we all just sat around and cried. It was pretty brutal around the school for a while after that.

After that Cape Breton high-school tournament, the Peterborough Petes of what is now known as the Ontario Hockey League (OHL) had some scouts watching me, and they were talking about drafting me. Because there weren't any major-junior teams in PEI back then, island teenagers were eligible to be drafted in both the Quebec and Ontario leagues. I ended up getting drafted in the first round by Sherbrooke and in the fourth round by the Toronto Marlboros.

Sherbrooke visited to sell me on playing there, and two Leafs legends, Johnny Bower and George Armstrong, came down to see me on behalf of the Marlies. They were offering a little bit of money—it wasn't a lot—and two trips to Toronto for my parents each year. But I came to see that Sherbrooke was a better fit. Sherbrooke had a population of about ninety thousand people, and I had been their first-round pick. Toronto had a few million people—a much bigger city than I'd ever lived in—and I was the team's fourth pick. Also, the Marlies had won the Memorial Cup the year before and they still had a good team, so I knew I'd have a better chance of getting ice time in Sherbrooke.

So, I was seventeen and about to leave home. No more party central, with all its drinking and arguing. I remember sitting down with my parents when I was a little older, probably after my second or third year playing pro. I told them I knew they were very gracious and welcoming people, in some ways I admired that their door was always open, but they couldn't keep going on like that; they weren't making so much money that they could afford to feed everybody and have them drink their booze. I remember my mother saying, "Our house is open to everybody and that's just the way it is." I thought, *Okay, if you're not going to listen to me, go ahead, spend all your money, and you're not going to have any left when you get older.* And sure enough, that's pretty much what happened.

My parents weren't perfect, but they were good to us, very hard working. But the weekends especially could get pretty rowdy.

I was happy to get out of there, other than leaving my girl-friend, Joyce, behind. She was an all-round great athlete, star of the school basketball team and the top-ranked women's player in the province. On our first date I watched her play, and then we walked to McDonald's. It had just opened. She wouldn't be long for PEI herself, though she wasn't as keen as I was to get away. She'd soon head to Acadia University in Nova Scotia, early matriculation, to get her bachelor's degree in physical education. I remember being at the airport, getting on the plane, looking out the window and seeing my parents waving. Joyce was there, too. She was in tears as she waved goodbye. *I will never live here again*, I said to myself. Of course, that sentiment softened over time. I did go back in the summer when I was playing junior. And when I turned pro and married that girl, we'd visit for a month or so each summer. When the kids came along, we'd go back for a few busy weeks each year and stay with her parents, so all the parents and relatives could visit and see the grandkids. I think PEI is a great place—now.

But as I sat on that plane, I vowed I would never live there again. That was my goal. I'm sure my parents' house wasn't the only party central in Charlottetown, because it was a pretty big party town. But setting that goal was my way of saying, *I'm going to make it.*

2

HERE WE GO! (SHERBROOKE)

I wasn't the biggest guy when I got to Sherbrooke. I was six feet, but probably only 160 to 170 pounds. With the way the game was played back then, I had to let the older guys know they weren't going to run me over and get away with it. My first fight was with Mario Marois, a future NHLer who was in his third year with the Quebec Remparts. We dropped the gloves—and he hit me about five times before I could throw a punch. I didn't know he was a leftie! But I knew that if I didn't stand up for myself, older guys wouldn't stop trying to intimidate me. I fought quite a bit and got beat up most of the time, but they soon realized the skinny kid was going to stick his nose in and go after the puck, even if he had to take a few beatings to make his point. That approach hurt sometimes, but it helped me a lot.

As a seventeen-year-old with the Castors (I had no idea a castor was a beaver until I got there), I was named rookie of the year in the Quebec major-junior league. That season, 1976–77, I scored

51 goals and had 110 points—pretty good numbers—and finished third in team scoring behind a couple of older players, Jere Gillis and Ron Carter. That's when I was pretty sure I could one day play in the NHL.

Our coach was Ghislain Delage. He was a funny guy but also a hard-ass. That was fine. In junior you need a forceful hand. You're seventeen, eighteen years old; you're at that age when you want to do your own thing. So you need that discipline. I looked at it in a positive way. Even though he'd yell at you sometimes, it was usually for the right reasons. We all knew that. Somebody had to be the boss if we were going to stay on track and improve.

I had played centre all through minor hockey, but a couple of Sherbrooke's right wingers got hurt early in that first year. They asked me if I would be okay moving to the right side, and I said sure, whatever you need. They put me on a line with a couple of older guys, Gillis and Mark Green. Both could really play, and things went well. After a while the coaches told me they were going to keep me there.

That first year, Sherbrooke finished with 40 wins (in a 72-game season). We had a strong team. Richard Sévigny, who went on to play in the NHL with Montreal and Quebec, was our goalie—and a good one. We had a big scare in the first round of the playoffs when Laval National took us to seven games, but we won the last game 7–0. The Remparts, who had future NHLers such as Michel Goulet, Kevin Lowe, Marois and Val James, who I'd play with briefly with the Leafs, finished with one more win and we met in the final. We won in five games, finishing them off in their building. Our line—Gillis, Green and me—had 27 points between the three of us in the five games of the series. In those playoffs, as a line, we scored 30 goals and had 72 points.

With that win, we were off to the 1977 Memorial Cup in Vancouver, to play the Ontario and Western league champs, the Ottawa 67's and New Westminster Bruins. It was exciting, but frustrating too. Not long after we arrived, my line with Gillis and Green got broken up. It started with the fact that New Westminster might have had the biggest junior team in the world. As a group, their guys were probably bigger than most pro teams, and this was their third straight appearance in the Memorial Cup (they made it the following year as well). They had only a handful of guys on that team who made much noise in the NHL, including Stan Smyl, who would spend his career in Vancouver (little did I know at the time that we'd soon be teammates), but that New West line-up dominated in junior. Meanwhile, Ottawa was stacked. They had Doug Wilson on defence, Bobby Smith up front and several other great players, and were coached by a legend in Brian Kilrea. Those were two good teams.

We were watching New West practise one day and, all of a sudden, the next day two of our centres mysteriously got hurt! Since I was one of the only wingers who had played the position, they put me back at centre. They actually asked me if I was okay with the change. As far as I was concerned, whatever was needed for the good of the team was fine with me—and another centre was what we needed.

It was a big deal, playing in the Pacific Coliseum in front of more than ten thousand fans each game. I'm seventeen years old, my family's there and we're playing the two best teams in the country, besides the one I'm on. The crowds were especially large, and loud, when we played New West. Not that they needed the boost. Our first game was against them, and in warm-up their guys were skating across centre, all the way to our blue line. We had one player, Mike Breen—a tough guy from Massachusetts—who told them to get back on their own side of the ice. That was fine until the opening faceoff, when the puck dropped and the game opened with a line brawl. I weighed maybe 165. *Oh boy*, I thought, *here we go*. Those were big boys.

In the end I had a decent tournament, but it would have been great to see how my regular line could have done against that calibre of competition. We may have had a better chance of winning a game or two, maybe. New Westminster won the Cup and we lost all four games—two to New West, two to Ottawa. Combined, they outscored us 19–7, but it was still a great experience, competing for a trophy that's now more than a hundred years old. And there were a few people involved that year who would later influence my life, such as New Westminster coach Ernie "Punch" McLean, who would coach me at the World Juniors, and my future roommate Pat Riggin, a third goalie loaned to Ottawa for the tournament by the London Knights.

The Memorial Cup was a highlight of my junior season, but playing in Sherbrooke was a good experience overall. There was a Catholic girls' school across from the rink, and it had an old three-storey building in which the priests used to live. That was our home. The location meant we could all walk to practices and games, which was a necessity, since Sherbrooke didn't allow any of its players to drive. A few years before I arrived, a player had been killed when the team bus crashed. After that, they made a rule that no one was allowed to even have a car. So they put us all in this building. You had a roommate; there was a kitchen downstairs where they had cooks; and there were a couple of women who did all the laundry. It was pretty neat. We had two TV rooms—one was French, one was English—and another room with bumper pool tables, stuff like that. There were only a few guys on the team, one or two, who couldn't speak English. Most of the Quebec guys came from around Montreal and were bilingual, and the Eastern Townships had a large English population, so language was never a problem for me with the team. It only became an issue when I went out to a store or someplace. My dad was from Gatineau and spoke French (he liked the idea of me playing in Quebec), but I never learned the language. In Sherbrooke, we all figured it out. And hockey was a language we all spoke, so the game was the same for all of us. We had fun.

During my first year with the team I earned a grand total of $19.21 a week, after deductions. We'd get paid on a Thursday and we played on Friday nights, but we never played on Saturdays. That was the day we'd go to the mall, which was a cab ride away. We'd pool our money, go to the corner store and buy some beer. We always went to Bishop's University, since a bunch of people from PEI went to school there. We'd jump in a cab—six guys with our beer—and go out there for the afternoon, watch football or do something, have our beers and head back home.

I attended an English-speaking high school in Lennoxville, Quebec, which is where Bishop's is located. But I was only at the school for a short time. The education system in Quebec is much different than in other places. Kids are basically finished high school at age sixteen. Then they have CEGEP, which they typically attend for two years before they can enrol in a Quebec university. So there I was, already finished grade eleven in PEI and doing work I had done back in grades nine and ten. I went to the principal's office, explained that I had done all of it already, and asked if I could be moved up a year. They said no, that it was going to take me three years to finish. I said, "Well, it's not." And I quit. That didn't go over very well back home. For two or three months, I took correspondence courses from my high school in PEI, and then I stopped. Needless to say, my parents weren't very happy, but there wasn't a whole lot they could do about it. They weren't there. They couldn't drive me every day and make me go to school. It probably didn't help that I was still not getting enough sleep, scared I'd embarrass myself by wetting the bed.

During my second year, the team got us ice time in the mornings. The guys who didn't go to school—some had already graduated—would be on the ice for an hour, an hour and a half, and then we'd have team practice in the afternoon. So I got to work on areas of my game along with four or five other guys, tipping shots from the point or taking quick passes from behind the net. I wasn't so much a stickhandler, so I'd work on finishing in tight. Those morning sessions helped me get better.

That second season, 1977–78, I played in the World Junior Championship, which was held in Montreal. It had just been made a formally sanctioned tournament by the International Ice Hockey Federation, and it was the first time Canada didn't send the defending Memorial Cup champions with a few additions but instead put together an "all-star" team. And it was a really good team. It was so good that Wayne Gretzky almost didn't make the roster, or so the story goes. Even though he was lighting up the Ontario league as a sixteen-year-old, management believed the roster should have mostly older kids, especially guys in their draft year. There was talk that he wasn't going to be invited to the selection camp in December.

But then Bill Derlago—who had scored 96 goals the previous season and was having another great year in Brandon, Manitoba—tore up his knee in an exhibition game against a touring Russian team, the night before he was supposed to go to Montreal. I'm not sure if that's what opened the door, but Gretzky was invited to camp, made the team and was the star of the tournament. Some called it a coming-out party for him. He played on a line with Tony McKegney and Wayne Babych, led the tournament with 17 points and was named the most valuable player. You could see how special Wayne was even as a sixteen-year-old, but I don't think anyone could have predicted he would be as great as he became.

The tournament was different in many ways back then. It wasn't as popular as it is today. There were only a few thousand fans for many of the games, but it was pretty cool playing European teams for the first time in my life. Canada had won bronze and three silvers in the first four tournaments, and going in, we felt we had a team good enough to win gold and knock off the powerful Soviets. We did well in the preliminary round, handily beating the United States, West Germany and Czechoslovakia. In the playoff round, we opened up against the Soviets and got off to a good start, but we managed to turn a 2–0 lead into a 3–2 loss. That one stung.

We bounced back to beat the Czechs 6–3 and then faced the Swedes. We had another good start before we fell behind, battled back and ended up losing 6–5. In the end, we had to settle for bronze. The Swedes and Soviets were so skillful, and they played as a five-man unit in a way we had never really seen. The Soviets won it all.

They had all their big guys back then, names you'd remember, like Sergei Makarov and Slava Fetisov. Sweden had a pretty damn good team too—Mats Näslund was playing, and he'd score 100-plus points and win a Cup for Montreal. We played pretty well. Like I said, we had some good players: guys like Gretzky, Bobby Smith, Steve Tambellini, Stan Smyl, Curt Fraser, Mike Gartner; our defence was Rob Ramage, Craig Hartsburg, Willie Huber, Brad Marsh, Brad McCrimmon; our goalies were Tim Bernhardt and Al Jensen.

We got to use the Montreal Canadiens' weight room as a dressing room. They took out all the equipment and put stalls in for us. We were using their shower, got to walk around their dressing room every day, and got to watch them practise pretty much daily as well. That was a cool experience.

I did okay in the tournament. Punch McLean, whose New Westminster Bruins had beaten Sherbrooke and Ottawa in the Memorial Cup the year before, was Canada's head coach, and his assistants were Gus Bodnar, who had coached Oshawa and been with some successful Toronto Marlboro teams, and Orval Tessier from Cornwall in the Quebec league. That gave us a coach from each of the three major-junior leagues. Every game, they played four lines in the first period. If it was a close game they would cut back to three lines, but they might take someone off the fourth line, mix them up, take the best nine forwards on that particular night. That was the idea, anyway.

I played on a line with Rick Paterson, a centre for the Cornwall Royals, and Patrick Daley, a left winger with Laval. We were never bumped up. Even though in half the games we might have been one of the better lines, we didn't get many chances to play in the third period. Helluva thing. I don't know if they picked the right team for that type of hockey. No offence to Stan, Curt, guys like that—they had good NHL careers—but in that tournament it was more free-flowing east-west type hockey, and they really weren't suited for that style of play. They played on a regular basis because they were Western league boys and Punch was the head coach. Back then, he wouldn't have known much about the players in the Ontario and Quebec leagues. We were frustrated, but Orval took us aside before we left Montreal to explain why we'd played such a reduced role. He told us that we shouldn't take it personally. I think he was even more frustrated than we were. Still, that was a great tournament to be a part of.

Back in Sherbrooke, our team racked up another great season —41 wins this time—but we still finished with just the fourth-best record in the league. We beat Laval in five games in the first round of the playoffs, but then lost to Michel Bergeron and his Trois-Rivières team, which had finished first in our division with 47 wins and went on to win the Quebec championship. I had a good season, finishing with 76 goals and 155 points.

My roommate at Sherbrooke was Charles Tuplin. He was a good guy, a tough player. After my first season, we had taken the train and bus home and he stayed with my family for a week or so. Chuck had met my Uncle Frank and spent a lot of time with him. When the second season was over, I went back to Charlottetown again. There was nowhere else for an eighteen-year-old to go. Chuck came by for a visit, and when he said hello to Frankie—who was blind, remember—right away Frankie knew who he was. It was amazing. My grandmother didn't have a phone book, she had Frankie. She would tell him a number and he would remember them all.

That summer, I mostly hung out with my two closest high-school friends, Burkie and Tiddler, Brian Burke (not the hockey executive) and Tommy McNally. I wasn't home much because I didn't want to be. We went to the horse races at least three or four nights a week, sneaking over the fence so we didn't have to pay. We might have a few beers before going to the track, but I don't remember ever being drunk at that age—even with the team, in Sherbrooke. But that's kind of where it all started, I guess. And it would ramp up during the following season, after I made a big decision about the next stop in my career.

3

BABY BULLS AND THE WRONG BROTHERS (BIRMINGHAM)

I learned quickly, when I signed with the Birmingham Bulls of the World Hockey Association, that for me the toughest part of pro hockey wasn't playing with men, it was hanging out with them.

I was nineteen years old when I signed with the Bulls. It was 1978 and I'd just finished two pretty good years of junior in Sherbrooke. I'd finished fourth in team scoring and could have played another season in junior, and likely put up some really good numbers before being eligible for the NHL draft at age twenty, but I decided to make the jump.

A little background to my decision. The Bulls franchise was originally the Ottawa Nationals when the WHA started in 1972, but they moved to Toronto after just one season. Under the ownership of John Bassett, whose father John had been a part owner of the Maple Leafs, they became known as the Toros and signed some older big-name players—such as Team Canada hero Paul Henderson and former Maple Leafs star Frank Mahovlich—and a talented eighteen-year-old Mark Napier. After three seasons in the shadow of the Maple Leafs, and having to pay a ridiculous rent to play in the Gardens, Bassett moved the team to Birmingham, Alabama, where they had a nice big rink and became known as the Bulls.

As an aside, the Toros had a winger by the name of Tom Simpson. He was nicknamed Shotgun because of his big slapshot. Anyway, during the Toros' final season in Toronto, Shotgun Tom scored 52 goals, so technically he was the first Toronto pro to score 50 or more in a season—he just didn't do it in the NHL and with the Maple Leafs! I'll take that.

After a couple of seasons down south there was talk of a possible merger between the WHA and the NHL, and the Bulls sold off some good players, including Napier; a nineteen-year-old Ken Linseman, who had also signed as an underage; and several others. But the merger didn't happen, at least not right away. Bassett suddenly found himself in need of players, and he liked the idea of signing juniors. They weren't eligible to be drafted into the NHL until they were twenty, so they were eager to get paid, even modestly. I'm sure he felt there would be a merger at some point. And at the very least, he was pissing off the NHL.

The year before I joined the Bulls, they were, under coach and general manager Glen Sonmor, the WHA's version of the Broad Street Bullies—the old Philadelphia Flyers. The team was the most penalized in the league, brawling all the time, and stacked with tough guys such as Steve Durbano, Dave Hanson, Frank Beaton... the list goes on. But there was a feeling that the Bulls wanted to play the coming season as less of a goon team and a little more skillful. Whatever—we kids were cheap help, but we were also pretty good.

Bassett signed seven of us: goaltender Pat Riggin (London Knights); defencemen Rob Ramage (London Knights), Craig Hartsburg (Sault Ste. Marie Greyhounds) and Gaston Gingras (Hamilton Fincups); forwards Keith Crowder (Peterborough Petes), Michel Goulet (Quebec Remparts), who was eighteen, and me. Six of us were Alan Eagleson clients. My parents had asked a sportswriter who he'd recommend and he said Eagleson. He had Bobby Orr. What kid wouldn't want Bobby Orr's agent (though I dealt with one of his senior staff, Bill Watters)? Goulet was the only one of us to have a different agent. Thanks to journalist Allen Abel of the *Globe and Mail* in Toronto, our group of seven became known as the Baby Bulls. We tried really hard to sign Wayne Gretzky after his appearance in the world juniors, but his dad, Walter, made him stay in the OHL. I played with Wayne in that junior tournament, and I'd get a brief chance to play with him again a few years down the road, but I can only imagine what it would have been like to be on a regular team with him—whether I played on his line or not!

At the time, people questioned my decision. Why go to a fledgling league and a franchise that had been on the move? Wait a year and get drafted into the NHL, they said. Well, it was a great opportunity. We'd had a pretty good team in Sherbrooke for two years, but Jere Gillis was gone, Mark Green was gone, Ron Carter was gone—all our top players I'd played with were gone. They were older than I was and had graduated. I'm looking at the team and asking myself, *Who am I going to play with? How are we going to do?*

And then this opportunity comes along. I figured I was going to get a chance to play against professionals and, more than likely, that would make me a better player. So that's why I did it.

I didn't sign for the money, that's for sure. Sherbrooke tried to talk me into staying. They really wanted me back, and they offered me more money than I ended up making in Birmingham (and back then the Canadian dollar was actually stronger than the US dollar). But I went with Birmingham—a $20,000 signing bonus and a $30,000 salary. I think all of us signed for $50,000. I kept telling Georges Guilbault, who was a co-owner and our general manager in Sherbrooke, that it wasn't about the money. It was about me becoming a better player and playing against better players. He couldn't understand it. Maybe he didn't want to understand it. He just wanted me there. George had lost a lot of good players and attendance was down. But Birmingham was the best place for me to play, so that was it: Alabama, here I come. No regrets.

Okay, maybe one or two.

My first roommate on the road was Paul Henderson. Maybe someone figured he'd be a positive influence on me. It lasted one night. My first game I scored, and after the game I went out with the boys. I don't know what time I got back to the hotel, but he was enraged. A reporter from PEI had been calling our room all night, waking him up, looking for me. I walked into the room, and he wasn't happy. Next game, I had a new roommate.

While there were seven original Baby Bulls, Keith Crowder left the team in November and went back to Peterborough because he wasn't playing much. So the six of us who were left hung out together, drove to the rink together, and lived together in the same apartment complex, which wasn't very close to where the other guys, especially the veterans, lived—maybe because we couldn't afford it. It was fun. We didn't make the playoffs, as there were six teams and only five made it, but it was still a great time.

I had been living with Crowder, but when he decided to go back to junior, Patty Riggin moved in with me. It was quite a change. Keith and I had gotten along really well. He was a great kid and we were great together. Then Patty came along. He was a good guy too. But he was a goalie, and goalies are different! On and off the ice, they have their quirks. He was really messy, for starters. One time, around the Christmas holidays, his girlfriend was coming to visit. I swear he hadn't washed his sheets from the day he moved in, and probably even before that. Even when I got on him about it, he still wouldn't wash them. So, one day he went out to do something. I got out the rubber gloves, went in, took the sheets off and washed them. I cleaned everything up. But when he comes home and sees what I've done, he gives me shit.

I said, "Patty, your girlfriend is coming tonight. Do you want her to sleep in that bed like it was?"

I did him a favour, and he wasn't happy about it. But once the girlfriend arrived and saw the clean room, well, I think he was happy after that.

The two of us were nicknamed the Wrong Brothers. There were the Right Brothers and the Wrong Brothers. Riggsy and I were the Wrong Brothers. Ramage and Hartsburg, who lived together, were the Right Brothers. How do I put it? They lived a little bit cleaner than we did. If you asked Bill Watters, he might tell you we were a bit of work, a couple of teenagers living like we were on spring break whenever we weren't at the rink. I started a fire by trying to make french fries in a frying pan and dropping the pan on the rug. Joyce came to visit. She wasn't impressed with any of what we had going on. We split up for a while. I never did learn how to cook.

I think it was our coach, John Brophy, who came up with those nicknames. The dressing room picked them up pretty quick. They were the good guys, we were the bad guys—the Right Brothers, the Wrong Brothers. A classic Brophism.

Broph was one of a kind. He was an assistant coach the year before with Sonmor, and that team, which set the penalty-minutes record, would have been one Broph loved. Over the years, he loved telling stories about the brawls he had been a part of. As a player, he was a hard-nosed, tough-as-nails defenceman from Antigonish, Nova Scotia, who played eighteen years in the Eastern Hockey League. He earned more than 3,800 penalty minutes in his career. He would have fit perfectly in the classic hockey movie *Slap Shot*, and, in fact, people have said that Paul Newman's character— Reggie Dunlop, the player-coach of the Charlestown Chiefs—was loosely based on Broph, who for years was a player-coach with the Long Island Ducks in the Eastern league. There was even a character in the movie named Nick Brophy. Our Broph was the league's all-time penalty minutes leader, but he was also a pretty good player. He went on to coach thirteen years in the East Coast Hockey League (ECHL) before he wound up in Birmingham, and our paths would cross again a few years later in Toronto.

I loved the guy right from the beginning. He could be a hard-ass, and he couldn't finish a sentence without swearing, but he treated us fairly. He pushed us to be better. He was good to us. He knew when we needed a kick in the butt and that extra push. I think he liked us younger guys more than some of the older guys—not that he didn't yell at us, too. He would throw fits in the room. But he pushed you, and I loved that.

I think the other young guys loved him as well. Probably some of the older guys didn't, because they didn't want to be pushed as hard, but that's fine. I liked him because all he wanted was for you to give him 100 percent of what you could do. And if you didn't, he would let you know it. If you did, he loved you and he played you. I guess you could say that about any coach.

Broph was very successful as a minor-league coach because he could push players to realize their potential. Not so much in the NHL. By the time he got there, times were changing. The use of video and systems was just starting to come into the game, and Broph wasn't a systems-type guy. He was more motivational.

After I retired, I coached against him. One night, I was coaching South Carolina in the ECHL and we were playing Broph's Norfolk (Hampton Roads) team. Broph put his tough guy on the ice. One of my tough guys was already on the ice and my guy beat the hell out of his guy. Broph flipped out and was screaming at me with his head around the glass. He wanted to fight me. I told him to relax, said something like "I'm not going to fight you, for Christ's sake. What's your problem?" His version of it was I sent my guy out after his guy. That wasn't the case. They were probably the toughest guys on the ice and they happened to be out together. He put his guy out after mine—I can't help it if my guy beat up his guy. It was kind of hilarious, and the players were teasing me about it because they knew I had played for him.

I remember one night with the Bulls. It was during an intermission. I was in the trainer's room, and I could hear these noises coming from down the hall in the weight room. I tiptoed down the hall, looked in and there's Broph, in his suit and tie, pounding the heavy bag, cursing away. He was so intense. And of course he carried that over into the dressing room.

Probably the funniest moment of the whole year, except maybe at the year-end party (Broph was there, too), was one night when we came into the dressing room after a period. We were losing, and Broph went around the whole room and gave it to every single guy, probably forty-five seconds to a minute berating each player on the team. Then he comes to Paul Henderson. Broph's standing there, just staring at Paul, and it's the only time I've seen him at a loss for words.

Henny was the hero of the 1972 Canada-Russia Summit Series, a veteran guy in his late thirties, and a born-again Christian. Broph didn't know what to say to him, because he couldn't say anything without swearing. When Broph got mad his voice would rise to a higher pitch, which it did suddenly, and he says, "Henny, maybe you can talk to the Big Fella up there, maybe he can help us, because the rest of these guys are no fucking good." Well, the rest of us in the room, we're choking back the laughter. You had to be careful because you couldn't let him catch you laughing. He'd probably throw something at you. We just buried our heads. And then that was it; there were probably five guys in the room he hadn't gone after, and he didn't even bother. He was done. He just left.

That year-end party took place at a bar across from the Civic Center, where we always used to go. The guy who owned it was from Canada. It was a narrow bar and there was an alley beside it, so when it was busy they would open the double doors and put tables outside in the alley. We were there all the time. The food was actually good. That night, Broph got pretty drunk. We all did. He was arm-wrestling us all at the bar and telling stories about his playing days—the brawling, guys hitting each other over the head with their sticks—and we're just sitting there listening. We couldn't believe the stuff he was telling us. All of it true. It was hilarious. But the more he drank the more he wanted to arm-wrestle, and if you beat him, then he got really pissed off. And he'd want to do it again and again.

Broph was actually the guy who gave me my nickname. It was by accident. We were at practice one day working on the power play at one end of the rink. Me being from PEI, everyone called me Spud. Broph's yelling at me to come down the ice, except he's screaming, "Squid! Squid…" Everyone's standing there, puzzled. Hartsy asked him who he was yelling at.

"Squid," said Broph.

"Who's Squid?" asked Hartsy.

"Vaive!"

"You mean Spud, not Squid."

"I don't give a shit what you call him, get him down here!"

When I was in Vancouver, I got called "RV," but when I got to Toronto, I ran into Hartsy when we were playing in Minnesota and he was with the North Stars. In the warm-up Hartsy comes up to me while I'm stretching at the red line and says, "Hey, Squid, how's it going?" I chuckled, hearing that name again. Dave Burrows was standing next to me and heard it. I knew right then—and I was right—that "Squid" would stick. It's with me to this day.

We had a lot of characters on that Birmingham team, guys like Jim Turkiewicz, Rick Adduono, Davey Gorman and Wayne Wood, our third goalie. Before warm-up, these guys used to play back-gammon in the area where you took off your clothes before you went into the actual dressing room to put on your gear. They'd be there playing for money before the game and I'm thinking, the first time I see it, *What the hell are these guys doing? We've got a game!* Welcome to the pros.

Then there was our captain, Brent Hughes. Broph started sitting him. That didn't go over too well. One night, Broph scratched him when my brother Steve, who was seventeen, was in town visiting. Brent told me he'd look after him, so he brought Steve up to the press box to watch the game. Well, in those days, they had a keg of beer in the press box. By the time I got showered and changed after the game and over to the bar, Steve and Brent were both half in the bag.

Dave Hanson was on that team. You might remember the famous Hanson Brothers in the movie *Slap Shot*. Dave was one of the Hanson Brothers—Jack. Steve and Jeff Carlson were the other two. I think that movie has played on every hockey team bus in North America.

Dave was a great guy. All our tough guys from the previous sea-son, the ones who'd beaten the hell out of everybody, they were gone: guys like Gilles Bilodeau, Frank Beaton and Steve Durbano, who was absolutely nuts. All those guys were tough and crazy and led the league in penalty minutes. Durbano had 284 penalty min-utes, Beaton 279, Bilodeau 258 and Davey 241. Of all those tough guys, only Dave was left. Unfortunately, some teams had long memories, and they decided to take it out on us. Dave did his best to protect us, but he wasn't on the ice that much. He played only 53 games, although he still managed 212 minutes.

I'd had my share of penalty minutes in junior. I always believed you had to stand up for yourself so guys knew they couldn't take advantage of you. I guess that same mentality prevailed in Birmingham, because I tied Winnipeg's Scott Campbell for the league lead that season with 248 penalty minutes. As I said, teams were coming after us—it wasn't all me initiating it. I got beat up a lot, had my nose broken a few times and took a lot of punches to the head.

One night I was playing in Edmonton. This was when the Oilers had Dave Semenko, a big, tough man. It just seemed like every time we played Edmonton, their coach, Glen Sather—who was a big-time chirper—would yap at me from the bench. He wouldn't shut up. Finally, I just said, "Would you shut up? Either that or put on your equipment and come out here." He said, "I'm going to send Semenko after you." I told him to go ahead. So Semenko came on. We're playing, we're skating up the ice, we both turn—he suckers me and then grabs me by the back of the sweater, hits me a couple more times and knocks me out cold. It was brutal.

I played a physical game and I answered the bell. After a while, I think guys got tired of breaking their knuckles and hands on my head, but I earned some respect and some space on the ice. And I did win my share of fights. I remember our GM in Birmingham, Gilles Leger, once said I was "naturally ornery." I don't know about that, but I hated losing—fights and games.

There were a lot of tough guys in the WHA, and the Bulls were a circus act the year before I signed. Broph used to tell a story about Dave Hanson getting into a fight with Bobby Hull. During the scrap he wound up pulling off the Golden Jet's hairpiece. Davey was standing there in shock with this toupée in his hand—he didn't know what to do. Then he just threw it to the ice like it was going to bite him. Hull picked up the rug and played the rest of the night with a helmet. There were nights when that league was a bit of a gong show.

The travel was brutal, too, and that wasn't good news for me. I hated flying—still do. It was especially bad after Indianapolis folded, only twenty-five games into the season. That's when Gretzky went to Edmonton. We're in Birmingham, in the Deep South, and we have to go to Edmonton, Winnipeg and Quebec. You can imagine. There were only two other teams left now in the US—Cincinnati and Hartford (New England)—and the latter were playing in West Springfield that year because the roof had collapsed at the Hartford Coliseum. So there were some really long trips. We'd leave Birmingham and we'd have to fly to Atlanta and stop in Dallas and go up to Minneapolis and then to Winnipeg. There were sometimes fourteen-hour travel days. So yes, the travel sucked. But I couldn't complain too much, because Birmingham had really decent weather. It would be the middle of October and still seventy degrees. Of course, the locals thought it was cold, and the apartment complex would close the pool. We're walking around in shorts and T-shirts, the locals are wearing jackets and I'm going, "Why'd you close the pool?" We'd still be swimming.

New England had Dave Keon, who was, of course, a legend with the Leafs, a captain who left Toronto on bad terms. (Little did I know...) They also had the legendary Gordie Howe, one of the greatest players ever, who was playing with his two sons, Mark and Marty. Gordie was fifty years old that season. Age didn't matter to Gordie. He was still good. And he knocked me out with an elbow one night. That was a funny story, kind of. The game was in Birmingham and we were up by a goal late in the third. Broph would use me on faceoffs in our zone, especially when the faceoff was on the right side. I was still good at faceoffs on that side, from playing centre as a kid. The Whalers had pulled their goalie. I won the draw and we iced the puck, but I beat their guy to the puck. I got it, came around the net and turned to put it in the empty net when—wham! Gordie was backchecking, and when he went past he gave me an elbow to the back of the head. I went down and couldn't get up. I kept trying and I kept falling. I started crawling to the bench and all I could hear was Broph screaming, "Get off the ice! Get off the ice!" because the Whalers were going back the other way. We ended up winning the game, so everything turned out okay. I actually didn't remember it happening, but the next day I looked at the game film and there was Gordie, skating back, and then all of a sudden as he went by me, I basically flipped over and landed on my head and was crawling off the ice. My badge of honour—Gordie Howe knocked me out. Pretty cool. I guess I wasn't really knocked out, but I sure was groggy. If it happened now, with concussion protocols, they'd have stopped the play and I'd be out for a month.

That season, we missed the playoffs by just two points, although Broph was named coach of the year. Even if we had made it, though, we would have been in tough. Edmonton, with Gretzky, finished first with 98 points; we had 70. But the Oilers lost in the final to Winnipeg, which had finished third, behind Quebec, with 84 points.

All of the Baby Bulls had had a good season. I led the team with 26 goals and 59 points in 75 games, and I had those 248 penalty minutes. I would consider that a good year for a nineteen-year-old playing his first season of professional hockey. Of course, the league probably wasn't as good as the NHL at the time, but there were still some damn good players. Goulet finished second in team scoring, Hartsy sixth and Rammer seventh, so four of the top seven scorers were from our little gang of friends, and Riggsy was our number-one goalie. I think we all developed more than we would have had we stayed in junior. I was glad I'd made the decision to play pro instead of returning to Sherbrooke.

Our owner, John Bassett, did something good for us that season, at the urging of my agent, Bill Watters. Partway through the season, when it was clear Birmingham wasn't going to be a team in the NHL after the leagues merged, Bill got Bassett to sign the young guys to good, long-term contracts—I believe they were four-year, $650,000 deals—expecting that the NHL teams that picked up those contracts would have to honour them as part of the merger agreement. Of course, Bassett knew he wasn't going to have to pay those salaries himself, so the contracts were no burden on him.

But I did get an additional amount, as did Rammer, Hartsy, Riggsy and Gingras. Bill launched a lawsuit against the NHL for discrimination, because—to put it simply—Gretzky had signed a personal services contract with owner Nelson Skalbania in Indianapolis that carried over to Edmonton, and as a result Gretzky didn't have to be part of the draft. He was an Oiler. The rest of us had to go through the draft, and that meant our NHL teams didn't honour those new deals Bassett had given us. Bottom line: the NHL settled with us. I think I got a $70,000 settlement, but we all still lost a lot of money. A lot of wheeling and dealing went on behind the scenes to make that merger happen.

That season might have been a lot harder without those other five young guys there. Playing with the Baby Bulls made it fun. There were nights when we'd just sit and talk. Having that support really helped, because none of us could go to the older guys—they would still be at the bar, the majority of them. Doing our own thing like that, and not knowing how to cook, we went out for most of our meals, which isn't the best thing for young guys. I think Hartsy and Rammer were a little bit better at cooking than we were. The Right Brothers ate at home a lot.

As I said, I discovered in Birmingham that the toughest part of pro hockey for a rookie wasn't playing with men. We were playing hockey, and we were good. Playing was the easy part. The toughest part was hanging around with the older players. We had ten guys in their thirties and we're all nineteen years old. There was quite a bit of drinking going on, and there was a fair amount of pressure on the young guys to be a part of it. If you didn't do it—if you didn't go out and get drunk with the veterans—you were probably going to get your head shaved again, or they were going to pick on you. After practice, it was lunch across the street, and if you didn't show up there would be trouble. So the six of us would go, have a couple of beers and leave, and that was okay. It was all about showing up. But then there were times when you'd go for lunch and get home at eight o'clock. The older guys often didn't want to go home to their wives, so every day, for them, it was lunch across the street and staying until eight or nine. We didn't want to do that, especially the day before a game. After games, it was different. We didn't worry so much, and the young guys would go out and party together. We probably partied a little more than I wanted to, or should have, but that's how we all lived at the time.

I really do wish I hadn't partied as much as I did. I think I could have been a better player. Soon enough, though, I'd get the chance to prove what I could do on a much bigger stage than Birmingham offered. The question remained: Would I make the most of the opportunity, or would I get caught up in the fun?

4

RED PLASTIC CUPS (VANCOUVER)

Pro hockey can be a humbling experience for a player. Chances are good that for pretty much all of your life—through minor hockey, then junior—you have been one of the best players on your team, if not the best. And then, all of a sudden, you get to the pros and that isn't necessarily the case anymore, at least to start.

That, in itself, can take you down a notch.

Finding yourself at the bottom of the pecking order isn't always because you're not good enough. Sometimes a player has to learn what it takes to be a pro. You have to grow up. Sometimes it takes time to mature as a person and a player. Once I got drafted, I needed to grow up—on and off the ice.

But my first taste of life in the NHL took humbling to another level. I got traded. Yes, a first-round pick of the Vancouver Canucks, selected fifth overall, and I got traded halfway through my rookie season. One day you're supposed to be the future of the franchise, the next day you're the past.

That I got to Vancouver in the first place was a bit of a surprise. The summer of 1979 saw the merger between the World Hockey Association and the NHL. Edmonton, New England, Quebec and Winnipeg were all granted expansion franchises for the upcoming season, while our Birmingham Bulls and the Cincinnati Stingers dissolved, though both owners received a handsome parting gift. Funny enough, Vancouver was one of the teams that initially opposed the merger, but later they changed their minds.

Anyway, the NHL put the screws to the four WHA teams, stripping their rosters of all but a handful of players and making them select at the end of each round in the draft. (Times had changed dramatically by the time the expansion Vegas Golden Knights arrived in the NHL in 2017!) Because the merger—or maybe *expansion* is a better term for it—was approved in late June, the draft, which is normally held in June, was pushed back to August 9, and it was conducted over the phone. Normally, teams and prospects would gather in Montreal at the Queen Elizabeth Hotel, but not this time. Prior to the draft, Vancouver hadn't spoken with me or my agent at all, which is one of the reasons I was kind of shocked when they drafted me. Washington had the number-four pick and had spoken with Bill Watters. I hadn't heard a peep from Vancouver.

That draft is regarded as one of the best in NHL history. After the merger, with a bunch of us young guys available from the WHA, the NHL lowered its draft age from twenty to nineteen, which effectively meant that there were three draft years eligible in one. On top of that, the NHL reduced the number of draft rounds from twenty-two the previous year to six, which was the fewest since 1971, when there were ten rounds. Needless to say, a lot of very good players didn't get drafted, and among those who did were a bunch of future Hall of Famers.

In the papers, there was talk that I was slotted number four, which is when Washington was drafting. Just to be selected, especially high in the first round, was a great honour when you consider the talent involved in that draft. As it turned out, my Baby Bulls teammate Rob Ramage went first overall to Colorado. A big left winger from the Portland Winterhawks, Perry Turnbull, went to St. Louis with the second pick. Mike Foligno, a right winger from the Sudbury Wolves, went third to Detroit, and then Washington selected Mike Gartner, a right winger who had played for Cincy of the WHA, fourth. That left me available at five for the Canucks.

All the Baby Bulls got picked. Craig Hartsburg went right after I did, sixth to Minnesota. After us, Michel Goulet went twentieth to Quebec, Gaston Gingras went twenty-seventh to Montreal, and Pat Riggin was the first goalie selected, thirty-third overall to Atlanta. I definitely think that year of playing in Birmingham helped our standing in the draft. Teams could see we were ready to play pro hockey.

Ray Bourque, a future Hall of Famer and Stanley Cup winner, was selected after three of us Bulls (eighth to Boston), so I don't feel too bad about falling from fourth to fifth! That Goulet was the second-last pick in the first round was a surprise. Some people, though, thought that was orchestrated—that as part of the merger, teams were told to leave Goulet alone so he could go to Quebec. I can't imagine that Michel would have lasted until the twentieth pick otherwise. He'd had a good year in Birmingham and he turned out to be a Hall of Famer, scored 600 goals. There was another rumour, that his agent had told teams he wasn't going to play for anyone in the NHL but Quebec. Regardless of how it evolved, they got themselves a great player.

A few big names fell deeper into the draft. Mark Messier, who had also been playing in Cincy, went forty-eighth to Edmonton. Guy Carbonneau went forty-fourth to Montreal. One name that was missing was Wayne Gretzky, of course. But, as part of the merger agreement that kept him out of the draft, the Oilers had to make do with the final selection in each round. They probably shouldn't have been given a first-round pick at all, considering they were getting Gretzky, but they were, and the last pick in that round was a defenceman from the Quebec Remparts who went on to have a great career himself: Edmonton selected Kevin Lowe twenty-first overall.

Because it was a phone draft, I stayed in Charlottetown to find out who'd selected me. I was hanging out with some old buddies from minor hockey as well as Burkie and Tiddler, at a place we called the fire hall (the firefighters used to drink there), just a little spot, complete with the jar of pickled eggs on the bar. When the phone rang and the bartender called me over, Bill told me it was Vancouver. I was surprised, since I'd been expecting to hear that I was going to Washington. Nothing against Vancouver, but it was the other side of the country. It was also such a long way from where the big things were happening in the hockey world, cities like Toronto and New York. I wasn't thrilled, but I thought, *Okay, I'll make the best of it.* After all, it was the NHL and I was the fifth overall pick. (I guess Washington did okay picking Gartner. He played ten seasons with the Capitals and went on to score 708 regular-season goals and get inducted into the Hockey Hall of Fame. Those ten seasons were about nine and a half more than I had in Vancouver!) And, of course, the Canucks didn't honour my Birmingham contract. Instead, they offered a standard NHL player's contract. Mine was $400,000 over three years plus an option year, $100,000 of which was a signing bonus spread over the three years. When I got my signing bonus, I bought my parents a stereo system, my sister a nurse's watch, and one brother a stereo, the other a TV.

I got to Vancouver, started training camp, and thought everything was going well. Then, little by little, things started to seem off. We were playing an exhibition game against Los Angeles and were up by three goals when this guy said he wanted to fight me. I can't remember his name for the life of me—he was kind of a tough guy, but not a heavyweight. I told him I wasn't going to fight him. It wouldn't make any sense. If he won the fight, it could change the momentum of the game. But I don't think Harry Neale, our coach, liked me doing that.

Then Harry started talking about my conditioning. One day, camp included a five-mile run, and afterwards, he was telling everyone that he beat me (which was a crock of shit) and that I was out of shape. Harry was probably two miles behind me. I'm thinking, *Don't start saying that shit.* Maybe he was trying to push me, I don't know.

He played me a ton during camp. We were playing a game in Vancouver, one of six in seven nights during the exhibition season. That night I was so tired, I got hit against the boards—not really hard, but my head hit the glass. I was wobbly when I got up. I was trying to get into the bench, but the guys were pushing me out. I was at the wrong bench. It's different now, of course, but back then, if you took a knock to the head like that, you'd sit a shift or two, and then it was back out you go.

I don't think I did anything to Harry. I don't know what I did to piss him off. He just didn't seem to like me as a player. He didn't seem to like Bill Derlago, who was their fourth overall pick the year before, either. When the season started, neither of us played very much.

Harry was a wiseass. He was funny, but he could get in his digs in a particular way—it wouldn't seem like it should offend you, but there was a zinger in there. He just started playing me less and less, all the while complaining that I wasn't in great shape, and eventually I ended up in the press box.

But that dig about my conditioning was far from the truth. My biggest problem when I went to Vancouver was not realizing the NHL would be so much better than the WHA. Maybe I went in with the feeling that everything was going to be fine. I had played well the year before—just went out and played hard—but it was a lot tougher, a lot harder in the NHL.

I don't know if my conduct off the ice got in the way with Harry. I think it might have. Not unlike in Birmingham, and later in Toronto, the guys used to hang out a lot after practice. The veterans treated the rookies and younger players well, and they always included us. I remember one of those vets was Curt Ridley, our goalie. He was married to a girl from Providence, and they fought like cats and dogs. He never wanted to go home alone. He would always invite some of us young guys back for dinner; that way, he wouldn't have to deal with his wife or end up fighting with her. He couldn't divorce her because he was worried her father would come after him.

I lived with Glen Hanlon and Brent Ashton in Glen's house in Burnaby, because there weren't a lot of apartments available in Vancouver. Gary Lupul and I finally found an apartment—it was actually next door to the building Harry was living in—but it was still under construction and we couldn't move in until later in the season. There were a few of us living in Burnaby, and Jack McIlhargey, one of our big defencemen, owned a bar there, so that's where we congregated. We hung out there quite a bit.

Harry always used to call me into the coach's room and talk to me about drinking. I said, "Harry, I go to Jack's bar with the guys. I might have a beer or two and that's it. I'm there because that's where the other guys are and that's where people my age hang out. I just go there to have fun. I'm not there drinking like crazy all the time." The bar was also close to Glen's house, so it was the convenient place to go.

But Harry seemed sure I had a problem. One night when he had me sitting out again, he heard from somebody that I'd been drinking from the red plastic cups in the press box. When I went to see the guys in the dressing room after the game, he accused me of drinking during the game (they had beer in the press box in those days). I don't know what I'd had to drink, probably a ginger ale. I certainly wasn't drinking beer during the game. We argued about it. "Don't you think you'd be able to smell it on me?" I said. There's ways to get rid of the smell, he insisted. There was no winning that one.

Vancouver was the first time since midget hockey that I didn't wear my usual number, 22. I thought it was cool in midget because the numbers didn't usually go up that high. I also just liked the way it looked, how the numbers covered the whole back of the sweater. But when I got to Vancouver, Bob Manno had 22 already. The team gave me 18. After a few months, when things weren't going so well between me and the Canucks, I began to wonder if that number wasn't bad luck. One of the young football players in PEI who died back in grade 11 had always worn 18. I asked to switch to 28. As it turned out, I'd get my 22 soon enough.

Lupul and I finally got our apartment. We'd just returned from a fourteen-day road trip, so we moved in and threw ourselves a housewarming party. We had a bunch of the young guys over. We weren't settled in yet—the phone wasn't even hooked up— but we wanted to kick back with the boys. The next morning at around 6 a.m., the phone beside my bed was ringing. I picked it up, thinking, *Wait a minute, the phone's not connected yet.* The phone line wasn't hooked up but the phone was plugged in—which meant the building intercom worked. The voice at the other end belonged to Harry, and he was asking me to buzz him in.

I hung up, thinking it was one of the guys playing a prank. The phone rang again. I realized it really was Harry, and I pressed the button on the phone to open the front door. Then I jumped out of bed and got Gary up and told him we had to clean the place, that Harry was on his way up. We're scrambling around, throwing stuff into cupboards, the garbage, anywhere, when the phone rings again. It's Harry. "Are you going to let me in?" he asks. I told him I thought I did, but he says never mind, just come down to the lobby.

So I got dressed and walked down. That's when he told me I was traded to Toronto, along with Billy, for Tiger Williams and Jerry Butler. I actually started laughing. I thought it strange that Billy, who was the fourth overall pick the year before, and me, the fifth overall pick prior to the season, were being traded so soon. Tiger had had some success with the Leafs, for sure, and he was a tough guy. Butler was a fourth-line type of player. I kind of laughed.

"What's so funny?" he said.

"Oh, nothing."

That was the end of the conversation. They'd made their decision. There wasn't much point arguing about it. I didn't even see Harry at the rink when I was picking up my equipment. That was it.

Billy said he got a call around 5:30 a.m. from Harry, saying, "I'm sorry to wake you, but you've been traded." Billy had replied, "That's fantastic!" Once the dust settled, we both felt it was a good move to get out of there, because we weren't going anywhere with the Canucks.

That wasn't the last time Vancouver traded away a top draft pick before he grew into his potential. You might recall a kid named Cam Neely. He was the Canucks' first pick, ninth overall, in the 1983 draft. After three seasons, they traded Cam—a future Hall of Famer—and a first-round pick (defenceman Glen Wesley) to Boston for Barry Pederson, who was a pretty good player. It ultimately didn't work out so well for the Canucks. But it sure did for the Bruins.

Years later, one of the newspapers in Vancouver rated the all-time worst Canucks trades: the Neely deal was number one. Ours was number two.

I ended up dressing for 47 games with the Canucks and had 13 goals, 21 points and 111 penalty minutes and was minus-12. Those were decent offensive numbers for a rookie, and there were a lot of minus players on that team. I scored my first NHL goal in my second game, against the Red Wings' Rogie Vachon, who I'd met in Charlottetown when he was with the Habs. It was a goal I don't normally score. I came down the right side and the defence-man was cutting me off, so I cut into the slot and backhanded one over his glove into the top corner. I left Vancouver with a half-season gone partly to waste, but at least I had the happy memory of that first goal.

Billy and I had to catch a one o'clock flight to Toronto. His wife, Kim, drove us from the rink to the airport. It's not like it is today, when players might get a day or two after a trade, or more, to get things sorted out before they travel to their new city. I just left my car at the apartment and paid for my brother and a friend of his to fly out to Vancouver and drive it to Toronto for me.

Billy and I were tight at the time, and we weren't. Billy was married and already had a kid, and he and Kim lived on the other side of town from where I was out in Burnaby, living with Glen and Brent. I'd see him at the rink, obviously, and we'd hang out on the road. A lot of nights we didn't play, so we'd be together in the press box, and we spent time skating together after practice. Billy was in Harry's doghouse as well. I guess we shared our miseries. We became pretty close after the trade.

Once the idea of being traded settled in, my mind started turning things over. *Holy shit, this is real*, I thought. *I might not have much of a career because I've already been traded in my rookie season.*

How long am I going to play? It's a scary feeling—and it isn't supposed to happen to guys picked so high in the draft. I wondered if one NHL team giving up on me meant others might worry I was a problem.

Looking back on it now, I can see it was a trade the Canucks maybe had to make. They had gotten rid of a few older guys already that year, like leaders Don Lever and McIlhargey, and they'd lost a lot of their toughness. They had to bring in a guy like Tiger. Years later, Harry said Tiger was the most competitive player he had ever coached. He also said he thought the team had been having too much fun off the ice. But we were good players; we just weren't ready. So why not send us to the minors and let us grow up a little? I still wonder about that.

Two years after the trade, the Canucks ended up going to the Stanley Cup final against the defending champion New York Islanders. Tiger played really well in those playoffs. Once I got out of Vancouver, I didn't hold the trade against Harry at all, or his decision to play me so little. (I can't say the same about my other trades.) I got along fine with him after that and still do. I never held a grudge. You come to understand that it's a business and shit happens. And while Harry certainly had a hand in the trade, the general manager at the time was Jake Milford, who had taken ill that season but still signed off on it.

Anyway, Billy and I made our flight to Toronto, but we weren't on the ground for long. The Leafs were playing in Long Island the next night and were already in New York, so we caught our connecting flight in the morning to join the team and be available for the game. Funny story: On the flight to Toronto, Billy says,

"Let's have a couple of beers and relax." We call the stewardess over, but then the pilot announces that it's election day in Canada and they aren't allowed to serve alcohol on the flight. Billy offered the flight attendant big money to serve us. I don't remember how much, but it was enough for me to tell him not to waste his money—we didn't need a drink that bad! Well, we didn't get any beer, and it was a good thing too. When we got to Toronto there was a ton of press at the airport waiting for us. After we did all the interviews, I turned to Billy and said, "I told you it's a good thing we didn't have any beer!"

5

A CHANCE TO PLAY (TORONTO)

After the initial shock of being traded by the Vancouver Canucks—
and the initial fear that my career might be in the dumpster only
partway through my first NHL season—things worked out pretty
well, and pretty quickly, at least for me.

Putting on that Maple Leafs sweater and playing at historic
Maple Leaf Gardens, that was special. There was always the smell
of popcorn in the air. And I can still picture that hallway from
the dressing room to the bench—what a feeling making that walk,
looking up and seeing all those fans. I grew up watching games on
TV on Saturday nights, either from the Gardens or the Montreal
Forum, and dreamed of one day playing in those buildings. And
the Leafs were on *Hockey Night in Canada* almost every Saturday
night, which meant that after the trade my parents, family and
friends could finally watch me play. That would have been a rare
occurrence if I'd stayed in Vancouver.

I had heard the Leafs were a circus that 1979–80 season
under Punch Imlach and owner Harold Ballard. News travelled

differently back then, but the hockey world was still a small one, and word got around. But as a young guy, new to the team, I didn't think about much beyond being ready to play. This was a big chance for me.

Punch, who had previously been with the Leafs as coach and general manager and had won four Stanley Cups in the 1960s, was fired in 1969 by team president Stafford Smythe, but Harold decided to rehire him as GM on July 4, 1979. And that was a turning point in Leafs history. Under GM Jim Gregory and coach Roger Neilson, who Harold had actually fired on TV the previous season and then rehired a few days later, the Leafs had put together a pretty good team in the late seventies, one that maybe just needed some fine tuning, or so a lot of people thought.

But when Punch came back he immediately announced that he felt differently, that only a handful of players were worth keeping, and that he was going to get rid of what he perceived to be a country-club atmosphere. He essentially blamed the previous management for the state of the dressing room, and he felt Darryl Sittler, as captain, had played too strong a role in allowing that atmosphere to set in. Punch signalled his intent to shake things up and then got right to it, which is how I ended up in Toronto.

Imlach didn't like Alan Eagleson, who ran the NHL Players' Association (NHLPA) and was also Darryl's agent—and mine and many others' at the time. To say the team was in disarray was an understatement. Punch clearly had Darryl, who had a no-trade clause in his contract, and Eagleson in his sights. Darryl has told the story that the first time he met Imlach, Punch said, "Who do you think you are?" and made it clear that the general manager was in charge, not the captain. The hostility escalated when Punch banned Darryl and goalie Mike Palmateer from taking part in the taping of a *Hockey Night in Canada* intermission segment called "Showdown." Harold and Punch tried to get a court injunction to stop them, but it didn't work. The team even got fined by the NHL. I was told the NHL used to have a bylaw that allowed the president to fine an owner $1 million if they ever took the league to court. I don't think that was the case this time, but it was a different league back then. After that, the relationship soured between Punch and Darryl, to say the least, and Darryl was very well liked in the room.

Punch got to work over the fall, and his initial trades struck players and fans alike as being made purely out of spite. It seemed he was trying to get at Darryl, especially when he traded Lanny McDonald to Colorado on December 29. Lanny—also an Eagleson client—was packaged with Joel Quenneville, who had been a high draft pick a year earlier, for forwards Pat Hickey and Wilf Paiement, who were both good players, but no Lanny McDonald. Fans were so upset, they protested outside the Gardens. Darryl, who was Lanny's best friend, was so mad he gave up the captaincy. That night, he wore the "C" in the pre-game warmup, but before the game he got a small blade and cut it off his sweater, and was quoted in the papers as saying, "They couldn't trade me, so they traded my best friend."

A few weeks later, Punch traded big defenceman Dave Hutchison, another of Darryl's pals, to Chicago. A bunch of guys got together to have a few beers and wish Hutch well, and someone pinned a picture of Punch to the dartboard in the bar. Of course, the media found out, and it was on the front page of the newspapers. That was just one of many nasty battles between Punch and the players that went public.

Trading Tiger Williams (and Jerry Butler) for me and Billy in February 1980 wasn't a warmly received move. Tiger had been a very popular Leaf and was also close with Darryl. Unlike some of the other moves Punch made, though, I think our deal turned out to be a good hockey trade, whatever the motivation behind it. Punch apparently loved former first-round picks. I had been selected fifth overall, and Billy fourth overall the year before me, and we were twenty and twenty-one years old respectively. If Punch was set on breaking up the old gang, he might have seen Billy and me as the faces of the future. Hard to say.

At the time of the trade, the Leafs were on a long road trip to play both New York teams, then Chicago, Winnipeg, St. Louis and Colorado. Next up was a home game against Philadelphia, and then it was back on the road to Detroit and Pittsburgh. Billy and I joined the team in Long Island the day after the trade. There was no press conference or any fanfare of any sort, just the reporters meeting us at the airport. When we got to the hotel, Punch called us to his room, sat us down and told us we were going to get a chance to play a lot: play to the best of your ability, keep your nose clean and everything will work out just fine. And it did work out pretty well for us, even with all the other crap happening around the team. They put Billy and me together with Hickey, who was a good guy, and we clicked.

I wore number 20 in my first game. Tiger Williams had worn 22, and I don't think the team had the equipment with them on the road to take the nameplate off his sweater and put a new one on. I told them I wanted 22 and they hemmed and hawed about it, maybe because it was Tiger's old number, but they eventually gave it to me. It's funny, Tiger had scored the last goal in the Leafs' win against the Rangers in New York a couple of nights earlier, and I scored twice in that first game in Long Island. I played pretty well through the rest of the season, too. I had nine goals and 16 points in 22 games. So, I was really looking forward to the next year, but also hoping the drama around the team would die down.

I've been asked over the years what I thought about the whole situation with Darryl and Palmy taking part in the "Showdown" segment, even though I wasn't in Toronto when it happened. As far as I'm concerned, it was their call. Mind you, I also feel that if your GM doesn't want you to go—in part because someone had gotten hurt doing it the year before—well, he's your boss. I probably wouldn't have done it. But that's just me.

As for the other drama around the team, well, sometimes it got pretty serious. Carl Brewer, who had played for Punch in the 1960s on a few of those Stanley Cup–winning Toronto teams and actually butted heads with him, came out of six years of retirement at the age of forty-one. Brewer had been a talented defenceman back in his day. Later in life, he was a key player in getting Eagleson out of the NHLPA and eventually charged by authorities in the United States. I think most of the players thought Carl had come back to serve as Punch's spy in the dressing room. Whether he was or not, I don't know. It was a strange decision, but at the same time Carl could still skate pretty darn well. He was probably the fastest skater on the team. A few of the guys didn't like having him around, though, and they didn't like playing with him. I remember one practice, we were doing laps and Ian Turnbull—who was not a fan of Punch—was leading the way, just ahead of Carl, who was catching up. As Ian went around the goal, he pulled the net off its moorings and Carl crashed headfirst into the post. He needed thirty stitches in his forehead. There was actually a piece of skin left on the post. It was ugly. There was some crazy shit that went on. Carl played okay for us, but after 20 games he retired for good.

Floyd Smith, who Punch had acquired as a player in 1968 when Frank Mahovlich (another victim of clashes with Punch) was sent to Detroit, was the Leafs' coach for the first 68 games of that 1979–80 season. Punch had Floyd coaching for him in Buffalo, when he was GM there. It was weird with Floyd. After the trade, Billy and I were staying at the Westbury Hotel, which was on Yonge Street a block from the Gardens. We'd go out for dinner, we'd come back and we'd have to walk by the bar to get to the elevators. Every night, there was Floyd sitting at the bar. He was still living in Buffalo, so he'd stay at the hotel when we had a busy schedule. He would start every practice by blowing the whistle. Everybody would circle in around him, and he'd tell us not to get too close because he had a cold and didn't want us to get sick. We could smell the booze on him from twenty feet away. He was injured in a car accident in mid-March and couldn't coach anymore, so Joe Crozier came in, and that got crazy.

Before Joe took over for the final 10 games, Dick Duff coached two games. Duffy is a great guy, and he had been scouting for the Leafs. But we lost both games and Duffy was crushed; he thought we'd given up on him. He damn near cried. We didn't quit on

Duffy. The other teams were just better. Then Joe came in, and he was old-school. At practice, he would make us skate the length of the ice, down and back, down and back, and he would sit on a chair watching—on the ice! He checked curfew pretty much every single night, and he picked a few battles the next season, including one with Darryl.

Then there was the time the next season, when we came back from a road trip to Los Angeles and Joe made everyone go to the Gardens to watch tape. Because we flew commercial, a lot of guys had bought booze at the duty-free on the way home. While Joe was doing his session, someone poured a big bottle of vodka into the Gatorade jug. Harold came in, drank a glass, turned around and said, "That was good," and then poured himself another one. Ian Turnbull used to torment Joe. One night, not long before he was fired, Joe was giving his pre-game pep talk, which was more of a tirade, and in the middle of it Bull rips off a loud fart. Joe just stopped talking and left the room.

Despite all the grief he had to endure that season, Darryl played well and led the team with 40 goals and 97 points. Börje Salming had a terrific year, too, second on the team with 71 points, including 19 goals. We were scoring a shitload of goals, but also allowing a shitload. That year, we scored 304, which was seventh-best in the league, but we gave up 327, which was the league worst and quite a drop-off from the previous seasons under Neilson, when the Leafs had been strong defensively.

Part of the defensive problem stemmed from the fact that we were burning through a ton of goalies. The year I got there, we had five: Palmy, Paul Harrison, Jiří Crha, Curt Ridley and Vincent

Tremblay. The next year we added Michel "Bunny" Larocque and Jimmy Rutherford, for a while, and in later years we had Donny Edwards, Rick St. Croix, Tim Bernhardt, Ken Wregget, Allan Bester... It wasn't all on the goalies, of course, but we had so many who were just okay. And then we started drafting good young defencemen and rushing them into the lineup, but that's another story.

Crha came over from the Czech Republic to play in that 1979–80 season. He wasn't really ready for the NHL, but they played him and he actually started the playoffs against Minnesota, which didn't sit well with Palmy. Crha faced 61 shots in the first game and we lost 6–3. Palmy played the next game, then Crha the third game, and we were swept by Minnesota. The next fall, during an exhibition game, Joe told Jiří he was going to play the second half of the game (I don't remember who started for us or who we were playing). He didn't quite understand how that worked. It was right about the halfway mark of the second period when a delayed penalty was called on the other team. Our goalie came to the bench for the extra attacker and Jiří suddenly grabbed his mask and gloves and was halfway over the boards. He thought we were changing goalies on the fly. Someone grabbed him and pulled him back.

A lot of things like that happened. It was crazy times, and we had a lot of characters. One night in Pittsburgh we were supposed to charter home after the game, but there was an ice storm, so we couldn't fly out. We went to this hotel by the airport for the night. The rule back then was you weren't allowed to drink in the hotel bar, but because of the weather Floyd said it was okay this time to go and have a few beers. Everybody had more than a few, and then, all of a sudden, Dan Maloney, who was a tough-as-nails winger, wanted to start arm-wrestling everybody. Billy's father had been an arm-wrestling champion, so I knew Billy was good at it. We started taking bets. He beat Maloney, Paiement, Turnbull—he beat all of them—and we walked away with about $300 in our pockets. The boys weren't very happy about that.

Many people will argue that Börje was Toronto's best defence-man of all time (at least while wearing a Leafs sweater), but what they don't know is how much he liked to party. He could handle it, though, and still play well, because his fitness level was off the charts. He often had parties at his home. I was looking for a beer one night in his kitchen and opened the freezer. The whole thing was filled with bottles of vodka. *What the hell is this?* I guess the Swedes like their vodka shots.

I remember one time in New York, when Mike Nykoluk was the coach. We were playing the next night. Mike used to have meetings in his suite at 10:45 p.m., which was fifteen minutes before curfew. It wasn't really a meeting. He just called it to make sure everyone was back at the hotel. So we're leaving his suite to go to our rooms and Börje asks, "Who's coming out with me?" We're looking at him, thinking, *What the hell are you talking about?* I mean, yes, it's our last time in New York this year, but we've got a game the next night. I hated New York. It was so crowded, and at night you'd be trying to sleep while the dumpsters were being slammed down and the sirens were wailing. I didn't even like Madison Square Garden. The ice was lousy because they had so many events. Anyhow, I don't know where Börje went that night, but he and another guy took off. The other guy got home at two or three in the morning, and Börje got home two or three hours after that—and we had a morning skate. Didn't matter. That night, he had a goal and two assists and was the first star of the game. What he did never bothered me, even after I became captain, because he could be out late and still be one of the best players on the ice every night. I just looked the other way, because I could always count on Börje.

When that first season was over, I was feeling pretty good about myself. We still had some good players, and I was thinking that if things would just settle down during the next season and let us come together as a group, we could start making things happen. But then the dismantling of the Leafs continued, as did the battles for Darryl. It wasn't meant to be, I guess.

In June 1980, Palmy was traded to Washington. His contract was up and he was looking for term and more money. Of course, the whole "Showdown" episode and the battle with Punch the previous fall likely played into that move. Harold was at his craziest that summer, telling the press that Darryl would never play for the Leafs again and that he wasn't going to be invited to camp. Darryl showed up regardless—he had a contract and would have to be paid—and then Punch had a heart attack in September. While he was recovering, Harold patched things up with Darryl, and Darryl started to wear the "C" again. Harold had told Darryl that Punch was gone as GM, so he accepted the captaincy back. But partway through the season Joe decided to criticize Darryl in the papers, so more drama.

I think Darryl became a little distant after a while, with everything that management was throwing at him. I can understand that, given how he'd seen his good buddies moved and had gone through the battles with Punch and Joe. He'd still come to lunch with the team and have a beer, though, and he treated us all fine. To his credit, he didn't let the drama bother him on the ice. He was second on the team in scoring that season, with 43 goals and 96 points, one behind Paiement. I'm glad that, over the years, Darryl's relationship with the Leafs was repaired by later regimes and he remains a face of the franchise, one of the all-time Leaf greats. He really was a tremendous player.

He was also one of the pranksters in the room. He nailed a few guys' shoes to the floor over the years. In hotels, he'd fill up a pail of water, lean it against the door, and the guy coming in would open the door and get soaked. I wasn't a good morning person and Darryl knew it. So did the other guys. I was always grumpy in the morning. Guys would do things to me because they knew it would piss me off. One day somebody—probably Darryl—tied my pant legs in a knot so tight it took me an hour to untie them and get dressed. He would do the same thing with your shirt sleeves. It was funny, looking back, but at the time I would get so pissed off. But once you leave the rink, it's over. It was good fun.

The drama continued that 1980–81 season when Punch fired Joe as coach on January 10. We were 13-22-5, and a lot of the guys had tuned Joe out. So the firing wasn't a complete surprise. Problem was, Punch didn't have a replacement signed, so Darryl ran our morning skate. Then, a few hours before game time, Mike Nykoluk, who had been doing colour commentary on Leafs radio, was hired. Mike had been an assistant coach with Fred Shero in Philadelphia. He was a soft-spoken guy, and it turned out he was good for my career—and good for the team, too, as we played better down the stretch with him behind the bench.

We were still horrible defensively, though, and ended up allowing 367 goals, which was worse even than the previous season. We met the New York Islanders in the first round of the playoffs and were swept in three games, outscored 20–4. I ended the season with 33 goals and Billy had 35, so we'd made good progress over what we'd been doing in Vancouver a year and a half earlier.

One of the sad parts of the season was Punch forcing Ron Ellis to retire. When I got to Toronto, my seat in the dressing room was between Börje and Ronny. It was kind of like one of those old cartoons, with the devil on one shoulder and the saint on the other. Ronny was fantastic; he was great to me. Börje was, too. But they were polar opposites in terms of personality.

Ronny's best days were behind him, and I think he would say the same thing, but he was such a gentleman and such a nice guy that it was hard to see him go. He was the only guy in our room who had won a Stanley Cup. I think Punch, who had coached him on that 1967 Stanley Cup–winning team, told him he could either retire or go to the minors. Tough way for a great career to end. Ronny was a good influence in the room. He knew what was necessary to win and what it was like to win. He would talk about it sometimes. Sadly, a lot of his wisdom fell on deaf ears, since the needless drama caused by management was sometimes matched by the behaviour of our players.

Rocky Saganiuk was a young, cocky guy on that team. One time, we were playing Hartford at the Gardens, and the Whalers were standing in the corner watching our morning skate. They were waiting to go on the ice after us. Rocky skated down the ice, put his knees on the top of the boards, grabbed the top of the glass and leaned over. Gordie Howe was standing there, and Rocky says, "Hi, Gordie, I'm Rocky Saganiuk, the new era." He took a lot of heat from us over that stunt. Another time, he was skating through the neutral zone when he turned his stick blade over, put the toe on the puck, and started yelling like he was a cowboy. We're all thinking, *Oh my gawd, what is this guy doing?*

There were a few nights like that over the years in Toronto, on and off the ice. They left me wondering, *What's next?*

6

AT THE TENDER AGE
OF TWENTY-TWO

The 1981–82 season was as forgettable as it was unforgettable.

In order...

Punch Imlach, our general manager—the guy who'd acquired Billy Derlago and me from Vancouver a couple of seasons earlier—had a heart attack and triple bypass surgery in September. Harold was quoted in the papers saying he wasn't going to bring Punch back as GM, which was news to Punch. Harold had apparently asked him to retire, or consult, but Punch wanted to be GM. So, Harold fired him and replaced him with Gerry McNamara. As turbulent as times were under Punch, he had promised Billy and me that we would get to play, and he'd kept his word. The change to Gerry was not entirely an upgrade.

Under Punch, the club had already started trading away the core group of veterans, otherwise known as the friends of Darryl Sittler, and the purge continued that season with Ian Turnbull, Laurie Boschman and Wilf Paiement all traded, and then Darryl Sittler himself, gone to Philadelphia.

At the tender age of twenty-two, I was named captain of the Toronto Maple Leafs.

And I became the first player in team history to score 50 goals in a season—finishing with 54. But the owner didn't seem to notice.

Oh yeah, we also finished with a 20-44-16 record, a whopping 56 points, and a .350 win percentage (the Leafs' worst since 1957–58), and we missed the playoffs.

What a season . . .

The return of Punch in 1979 had surprised people around the team, given that he'd been away so long. And he'd come in guns a-blazing. But we knew Harold had a soft spot for him. Punch had won four Stanley Cups in the 1960s, so the owner figured maybe he could do it again. But times had changed, and Punch hadn't. It was different when Gerry took over, because nobody really knew who Gerry was. He was a former goalie, had played a game or two with the Leafs and had been in their farm system. He was a Leafs scout when he got the GM job. Many figured he was hired simply because he was around and would work cheap, which mattered a lot to Harold. And he wouldn't give Harold any grief, which also mattered a lot.

We were headed into my second full season playing with Billy and being in Toronto, so I was feeling comfortable on the ice and around the Gardens. We had bought a house the year before and Joyce lived with me that first season, while studying for her bachelor's in education at the University of Toronto. Then we got married in the summer. Everything was nice. We were settled, and I felt pretty good going into that season. But I wasn't aiming to score 50 goals, or even thinking I might score 50 goals. I was just hoping I could either repeat or maybe improve on my totals from the previous season. Keep getting better, don't regress—that was always the goal.

Even with Punch gone, there was still the undercurrent of Darryl and Harold fighting, even though it was Punch who had been front and centre in that battle. This was a bit of a distraction because everything was so public. I wasn't walking in Darryl's shoes, so I don't know exactly how the events of the previous two years had impacted him, but it couldn't have been easy. With Punch gone, it's possible Darryl thought things would settle down and that he'd be able to renegotiate his contract, but Harold seemed to stall him on that front and I think Darryl realized it wasn't going to happen. By December, a lot of people felt his exit was inevitable. That's what Harold wanted.

I didn't have many conversations—or any meaningful conversations, at least—with Harold, but I did see him in the dressing room every morning. Guy Kinnear, who was our trainer, would start the day by rubbing down Harold's legs to help with the circulation problem caused by his diabetes. So, our owner was taking up the trainer's time and the trainer's table every morning when we showed up for practice or a morning skate. If you wanted to get anything done by Gunner—get your wrists taped, anything—you had to wait until he was done with Harold. Harold didn't have much to say to us during those times, beyond maybe hello.

On November 11, before anything happened with Darryl, Ian Turnbull—who in 1977 scored five goals in a game (on five shots), an NHL record for defencemen that still stands today—was shipped out. That wasn't a surprise, and not just because of the team's movement away from friends of Darryl. I think Ian was pushing to get himself traded. I believe he had some tax issues in Canada and wanted to get out of the country and play in a US city. He'd also become a target of the Leafs faithful and was booed almost every night.

We were playing in Colorado and were out for dinner at a restaurant called the Colorado Mining Company. I'd had a thirty-two-ounce prime rib that night. When we were leaving—the brass were all there having dinner, too—Ian was sitting in an armchair in the lobby relaxing with a big glass of cognac, which was kind of surprising because it was quarter to eleven and we were all getting cabs back to the hotel in time for curfew. Ian decided not to sweat it that night, and he was still sitting in that big comfortable chair enjoying his cognac when the brass walked out. The day before, Mike Nykoluk had told the press that Ian would never play for the Leafs again. Ian had taken the coach at his word. A few days later, he went to Los Angeles in exchange for Billy Harris and John Gibson.

Billy had been a junior star with the Marlies and went first overall to the New York Islanders in the 1972 draft, the team's first season in the league. He had some good NHL years but was never the star player he was in junior. He was later part of a trade that brought Butch Goring to the Isles. Many believed Goring was the missing piece that helped them win four Stanley Cups in a row. There was talk that there had been a trade arranged to send Darryl to the Islanders, but Harold nixed it, and that's when they went and got Butch.

Not long ago, Billy was quoted in the *Toronto Sun* talking about returning to Toronto, saying, "I saw how poorly the organization was run. The first time I saw a scouting report on an opposing team it looked like a Grade 5 student had drawn it up. I'd come from years of playing under Al Arbour on the Island, one of the most organized coaches in the game. And (the Leafs) were asking me 'how did Al run his practices?' It's like the old saying, the trouble starts at the top."

Our team that season was incredibly young in goal and on defence. I remember the game on December 31, 1981. We beat Detroit 5–2 with five underage defencemen in the lineup (Jim Benning, Bob McGill, Fred Boimistruck, Craig Muni and Darwin McCutcheon) along with Barry Melrose. Flying home after the game everyone was in a good mood, but Darryl wasn't happy. He played the next home game on January 2, but left the team as we headed for Minnesota on January 6.

Darryl had asked to be traded in November, but his no-trade clause meant he could basically pick his destination. At that point, he had a letter from a doctor saying that he was unable to play because of the stress. He'd continued to play for a month, but come the New Year, the drama of Harold's Maple Leafs had pushed him to the brink. So he left. I didn't talk to him when it happened, but I remember thinking that he shouldn't have done that. I thought he should have asked for a trade, waited it out and kept playing. Looking back, I don't know what was going through his mind. I can't pretend to know what he was thinking or feeling. I'd been in the coach's doghouse in Vancouver, but Darryl had been in a years-long war of wills with one of the most difficult owners in the NHL.

There were just two teams on Darryl's list: Minnesota and Philadelphia. That left the Leafs without much leverage in making a deal. Finally, on January 20, Gerry traded Darryl to the Philadelphia Flyers for Rich Costello, a second-round pick who turned out to be Peter Ihnačák, and future considerations, which became Ken Strong. Years later, I heard that Punch had turned down a deal with Philly that would have landed Rick MacLeish and André Dupont in exchange for Darryl. That would have been a much better deal.

I think everyone was relieved that the saga was finally over, even though we didn't get much out of the trade. It didn't help us that Darryl wasn't playing either—he'd put up nearly 100 points in each of the past two seasons. But at least we didn't have to read about the drama in the papers or hear about it every day. And getting out of Toronto was no doubt a big relief for Darryl.

But with Darryl gone, no one was sure what would happen with the captaincy. Next thing I knew, I had it.

A lot of people thought naming me was a knee-jerk reaction by Harold, Gerry and Nykoluk. Harold just approached me one day in the outer area of the dressing room and said, "You're our captain." He didn't ask me; he just told me. The coach announced it in an interview that night, but that was all the notice my promotion received. So, just like that, I was the twelfth captain in the history of the Toronto Maple Leafs, joining the likes of Darryl, Dave Keon, George Armstrong, Ted Kennedy and Syl Apps.

I remember thinking, *This is fabulous.* It was a huge honour—there's no question about it—and I recognized it at the time. But I was just twenty-two years old and not sure I was ready to take on that role. I didn't know how the other guys were going to react. *If I could wait a couple years I'd be more ready*, I thought, *but if I turn him down he'll probably trade me.* That was the last thing I wanted. So I just said, "Thank you, Mr. Ballard. I'm honoured, and I'll do the best job that I possibly can."

I think Harold had asked Börje a couple of times to be captain, probably when Darryl gave up the "C." But Börje always said no. He didn't want to be the captain. Börje also knew he could say no because Harold loved him; he wasn't going to get mad and trade him. He would have been the logical choice. I think over time Börje probably regretted it, but he was also happy to be an assistant captain and not have to talk to the press every day, which is probably one of the bigger reasons he didn't want it.

I know that years later, when Mats Sundin was asked to be captain, he spoke with Börje, who told him to accept it, that it was something he ultimately regretted not taking, because it was the Toronto Maple Leafs, not the Arizona Coyotes or the Florida Panthers—not to diss those teams and their captains. But this was the Leafs, and it's a helluva honour.

This was the first great Catch 22 of my career (the fact that I was twenty-two years old at the time is just a coincidence): I know I'm really not ready to be captain, but if I say no I'll probably get traded and never get a chance to wear the "C," or even an "A," in one of the most historic franchises in the NHL, which I really wanted to happen someday. So I'm the captain of the Leafs, ready or not.

Looking back, I think wearing the "C" ultimately made me a better player. Once that letter is on your jersey, there's more pressure to be better. You are the captain and all eyes are on you. But at that age, it's tough to speak up in the dressing room and realize some of the older guys are ignoring you. No one was confrontational about it—the decision had been made, after all, and I was captain—but I'd see that look in their eye, like *Why are you talking?* Börje was different. He worked his ass off. I respected him and vice versa. Also, we sat beside each other in the room, and if I spoke up, he would say, "Yes, listen to him, he's right." But ultimately, I had to lead the way. Every day I had to do whatever it took to be the best player, so the others would follow. They couldn't question results. The more pressure there was, the better I felt I played— and my stats would soon bear that out.

I figured we could be a good team in a couple of years if we added some guys. We did draft some good players, but they were put into situations that didn't help them along, and the coaching—with all due respect to the guys who coached me, five guys in seven years—didn't keep up with the changing times. We didn't have systems. We'd do video, but they'd only point out the negative things, never the positive. There wasn't a planned forecheck; it was dump it in and chase after it. In our zone, it was a dog's breakfast, no direction. We didn't practise the power play or penalty kill that much. The power play was us just using our skills and imagination while moving the puck around.

I talked to Wendel Clark about this recently. I asked him what it was like in 1993 and '94, when the Leafs were good and got to the conference finals. He said it was pretty wild, as you would expect. He also said he thought that we had better teams in 1985–86 and 1986–87, when he first arrived, but we didn't have the calibre of GM and coach that we needed. I was surprised he said that. Then

I looked at the rosters. I believe we did have better personnel. Unfortunately, Harold wouldn't pay for a seasoned general manager or a coach who would come in and apply systems. Ultimately it came down to money with Harold. His bottom line was counted in dollars, not wins.

We knew trading Darryl and Turnbull was inevitable; they both wanted out. Pat Hickey was close to thirty, so trading him made some sense. Wilf Paiement was a good player for us, so it was a surprise that he got traded for Mirko Frycer. Laurie Boschman, a former first-round pick, was also moved. Harold was dumping some of the bigger contracts. As a team, we started getting younger —guys like Russ Courtnall, Gary Leeman, Steve Thomas, those guys would soon arrive—and it really looked promising. It wasn't going to happen right away, but you could see that maybe two or three years down the road we could be a contender. But because of Harold, we didn't hire the right GM and coach, and we never became the team we could have been.

The talent we did manage was, as I mentioned, good, but it was also mishandled. Benning, with all due respect, probably had the physical and mental attributes of a sixteen-year-old when he was eighteen and should not have been playing in the NHL. He would have been better served going back to Portland for another year or two. Freddie, same thing; even Gary Nylund. He had the physical attributes but not the mental attributes. There's nothing wrong with going back to junior and being the best player in your league, or in the country. That's going to help your confidence and make you better. But the Leafs rushed those young players along and made a lot of mistakes in their development.

It was a tough year because of that. We allowed 380 goals—dead last in the league. We had a young goalie, Vincent Tremblay, appearing in 40 games, although he split duty with a veteran in Bunny Larocque. Bunny might have been our best player that season. But with a young defence it was tough. We had to outscore teams to win, and we didn't have enough offensive depth to do that.

That's how you end up with turmoil and headed toward a 56-point season—15 points fewer than the previous year. We endured a stretch of 24 games, from late January to mid-March, in which we won twice. But there was at least one bright spot on the horizon, though I didn't see it coming.

It was probably about the time I scored my forty-third goal—we had 11 games left in the regular season—that someone in the press mentioned to me that I could become the first player in Maple Leafs history to score 50 goals in a season. I was shocked to learn that no one had ever done it. I had no idea. I just assumed that with all the greats who had played in Toronto over the years, someone had done it. Turns out Frank Mahovlich was the highest, at 48, a record he set in 1960–61, a seventy game season.

The press kept asking me if I felt any pressure to reach 50. I didn't. I heard stories about Frank getting to 48 goals with 14 games to go in the season and then drying up. But that didn't faze me. I always put pressure on myself, more than I ever felt from the outside. I just went about my business. If I was going to score 50 goals, it was meant to be. If I didn't, it wasn't meant to be. It was that simple.

But whenever someone mentioned it to me, I still thought, *Wow, it would be really cool to do that.* It was exciting; I just didn't worry about it.

It's funny. I had quit smoking that summer, and going into the season I scored twice on opening night in Winnipeg, had another the next game and four goals in the first five games. But I went seven games without a goal and had just nine in those next 15 games—so I had 14 goals after 30 games. I started smoking again, and the pace picked up. A lot of us smoked back in the day. We'd be in the washroom between periods lighting up, and after games or practices we'd be in the equipment room lighting our darts with the blowtorch we used on our sticks. Different times.

We played on the road a lot to start the season, and my first 10 goals all came away from Toronto. My first goal at the Gardens that year was on December 2, our twenty-fifth game. But then I got hot for a stretch from mid-December to New Year's. I had four two-goal games in a row and a total of 10 goals in a seven-game stretch. I went dry again and then started scoring at a fairly regular pace, with a few more two-goal games and a hat trick. I always seemed to be scoring in spurts. I had 24 goals midway through the season, but quickly added eight goals in the next seven games.

I was at 45 goals after 72 games, so I had eight games to get five more. In our next game, we got spanked 7–0 in Winnipeg. The game after that, at home against Chicago, I had a four-goal night against Tony Esposito. By that point in his career, he had bad eyes and couldn't see shots from outside the blue line. I got two from out there. Hey, they still count. Actually, I only put three behind Tony. The fourth was into an empty net—a club record number 49.

Lo and behold, the next day at practice the Big M—Frank Mahovlich—came down to the Gardens to congratulate me and have pictures taken together. That was really special, and what a great gesture on his part. He is a wonderful man.

Now I had six games left to get number 50, and I had a hot stick. I liked my odds. People ask: When you're hot, does the net look bigger? It did. It just looked like there was more room to score, and it seemed like everything I shot would go in. It wasn't so much *am* I going to score tonight as *how many* am I going to score tonight. That's how confident I felt.

The very next game—two nights later at Maple Leaf Gardens, March 24, 1982—I scored number 50 on the power play at 14:57 of the first period. Billy Derlago was, as usual, my centre. We had great chemistry, going right back to our half-season in Vancouver. I remember the goal vividly. When you're the first to do it in team history, you don't forget. Billy was at their blue line and got a pass from Benning. Billy skated across the line, deked one defender and deked another guy. I could see where he was going, so I got myself open on the opposite side—my wrong wing—and he threw a beautiful backhand pass across. It was pretty much just a one-timer for me. I had half the net to shoot at. Normally, I didn't miss those. Billy made a hell of a play on that goal.

I still have a picture of the goal. The Blues defenceman was the great Guy Lapointe—I'd kind of forgotten he was in St. Louis, after all those great seasons in Montreal—and he was down trying to block the shot. Mike Liut was the goalie and was desperately trying to come across to make the save. It didn't happen. The puck went in. Number 50.

And just like that it was over. I didn't have to think about it anymore. It's impossible not think about what you can achieve when something like that is in front of you. In the post-game interview, I said, "It's a big relief. Score that one tonight, a big piano fell off my back that I have been carrying around for a while. It's a great thrill. I'm just glad it's over with." That was a pretty special night, obviously. I had a few family members at the game: Joyce, of course; my sister Barb and brother Steve; and my Uncle Dave and Aunt Barb from Hamilton. I was so happy for my linemates—Billy and John Anderson—and all my teammates, the guys who made it possible for that to happen. It was a special night for all of us.

After the game, four or five of us and our wives and my family that were visiting went up a block on Church Street and had dinner at Bigliardi's steak house to celebrate. I had a nice big steak. After dinner, we went downstairs to the bar. The bartender started serving us a drink called a Green Lizard. It was a shot—one ounce of 151 proof rum and one ounce of something called green chartreuse. He had us sit in a barber's chair and gave us the shot. The girls didn't have any. The guys were already polluted when the bartender started serving those shots, but then he just put the bottles down on the table and left them with us. We closed the place.

It was a big night, an emotional one. I had worked hard throughout my career to improve, to become a good (and defensively responsible) goal scorer. Believe me, I paid the price in front of the other team's net. From the time I was a kid, I loved shooting pucks. I'd stay on the ice after practice and shoot. Then there were all those mornings practising shots and deflections in Sherbrooke. I guess it all paid off.

Of course, as wonderful as it was to reach that number, it happened on a team and during a season that was full of turmoil. After

I scored the 50, Harold didn't say anything to me. He never shook my hand or congratulated me. He told Gord Stellick, who worked in our front office, he was happy I'd gotten the goal, and so I had to hear it from Gord. But the club didn't acknowledge it in any way. In previous seasons, when Darryl had his 10-point game and Turnbull had his five-goal game, the Leafs gave them sterling silver tea service sets. Someone told me later that the reason Harold didn't do anything for me, or say anything, was because he was still bothered that he gave Darryl the silver tea set and then Darryl demanded a trade. That had pissed him off, and he didn't want to make a gesture like that again. I don't know if that was true, but all I got was the puck and a nice plaque that Toronto mayor Art Eggleton gave me from the city.

I do have one other keepsake to remind of the night, one that I have to admit is pretty special. Joyce had a ring made for me. I still have that ring. It's beautiful. I think she was more upset than me that the team never did anything, and she wanted me to have something down the road to remember that night by. And I do. I'm so glad she did that.

I wouldn't say I was upset with Harold, but I was disappointed. I'm still disappointed that something so special was allowed to just disappear into history, but at the same time I wasn't going to let it drive me crazy. On the twenty-fifth anniversary of the goal, the Leafs had a scoreboard tribute and invited me to sign autographs before the game. I enjoyed that.

In March 2020, I got back the stick I scored the goal with. It had been in the Hockey Hall of Fame's collection. For years I'd thought about getting it back, and maybe one day auctioning it off for charity. I'm not sure what I'll do with it. I let the Hall keep the two sticks I scored my other two fiftieth goals with. The stick I used at the time was a Titan Ultraglass TPM 2020. It hardly had any curve. I pick it up now and, man, is it heavy. Back in the day, some of my teammates used to called it "The Log" or "Big Bertha." The guys couldn't believe I used it. But I was breaking sticks like crazy; they weren't stiff enough for the way I played. The only way to make them stiffer so they wouldn't break easily was to make the shaft thicker. It was almost square. I remember playing an alumni game and a guy brought a stick for me to sign and it was one of my old ones. He looked around the room and said, "Can you believe this guy scored 50 goals three times with this piece of lumber?" Hey, it worked. I wasn't going to change it.

I got a couple gifts from outside the team after scoring the 50th. The guys used to go for lunch after practice to a restaurant on Adelaide Street called Mr. Greenjeans (it's no longer there). They had these big thirty-six-ounce steins of draft beer, the great big mugs. One day, the manager told me that if I scored 50, he was going to give me fifty of those huge drafts for free. So after the season was done, we phoned a bunch of the guys—Billy Derlago, John Anderson, Börje Salming . . . there were probably six or seven of us and our wives—and went there one night to cash in. I said to the manager, "We're not going to be able to drink fifty of those steins in one sitting, but can you give me the equivalent in dinner and drinks?" We didn't pay anything that night and had a nice celebration. The best part about it was I had those guys, my good buddies, with me. There were ten 50-goal scorers in the NHL that season—Gretzky, Mike Bossy, Marcel Dionne, and Bryan Trottier among them—and those greats surely all knew something I was glad to remind myself of that night: you don't set records like that by yourself. Canadian Club, the whisky company, sent me a three-foot-tall gold bottle engraved with congratulations. It wasn't a gift I needed, given the way my drinking was creeping up on me, but I've always appreciated the thought behind it.

I scored in each of the next three games and notched number 54, which still stands as the club record, in Philadelphia on the final night of the season, my seventy-seventh game. But that final night stood as the exclamation point for the 1981–82 season for all the wrong reasons. For Harold Ballard's Toronto Maple Leafs, it was time to come back down to earth.

Harold had arranged that after the game we would bus to Atlantic City, which was about an hour from Philly. Our plane was going to meet us there. I think the casinos closed at four in the morning. I still remember that in the couple of weeks leading up to that final game, a lot of guys went down with groin injuries, sore backs—the types of injuries doctors can't see and have a hard time verifying. We had I don't know how many guys sitting in the press box that night, just waiting for the bus to leave for Atlantic City. They weren't going to miss the night out, but they sure weren't going to play that game. You never knew if a guy was pulling the chute because he didn't want to play in Philly (back when they were the Broad Street Bullies we called it the "Philly flu"), but nine or ten guys going down the last week or two before that game? That was weird. Finishing so far down in the standings, you would have thought guys would want to play, to put on a good show and feel good about themselves before ending the year and taking that team trip. But the lack of standing room in the press box said a lot about the team, the character of some of the guys, and how they felt about playing for the Leafs. That was disappointing.

There was a sense among the players that the people upstairs weren't doing enough for us to be successful. You hear it all the time: if you want to succeed as an organization, you need to put your people in a place where they can succeed. But it felt like we were always putting guys in positions to fail, whether it was young guys rushed into the NHL or any of us without the scoring support of the great players we'd lost to trades to save money. So we weren't happy. A few of the guys didn't pull their weight, but most of us strapped on the skates and did our job, even if we knew there would be no help from up top or behind the bench. And that was never going to change as long as Harold was there.

Still, it's too bad the season had to end that way. Harold was doing what he thought was a nice thing—and it was—but it was also the wrong thing. Play the game, fly home, end of season: no rewards were necessary for a season like that, especially after the absolute embarrassment of the game we were about to play.

We lost 7–1, a real kick in the ass. I scored on a slapshot from the top of the circle, and that was the closest shot we had all night, because no one would forecheck or go near the Flyers' net. With that depleted lineup, we were terrible. Philly outshot us 59–18.

So, after all the turmoil and all the trades, everyone was a year older and another season of their careers was in the books.

Oh yeah, and Darryl had five shots and assisted on the first goal in that 7–1 beating.

Man, losing sucks…

7

FIFTY IS A BIG NUMBER

Setting records gets you attention. Not all of it is welcome. That summer, Alan Eagleson, lawyer, player agent and architect of the Canada Cup—and one of the most connected people in hockey until his fall from grace (and prison time) in the late nineties—came to our house and took Joyce and me out for dinner. It was an aggressive sales pitch at a very nice steak house called Barclay's. He said he'd always had the Leafs captain as a client and that he could make me more money than I was getting. He badmouthed my agent, Bill Watters, and tried to sell me on going with him instead.

We were flattered, of course, but not necessarily convinced. When I was playing in Vancouver, I was Bill's client, but Bill was part of Eagleson's agency, Sports Management Ltd. Over the season, Eagleson would visit all the teams on behalf of the NHL Players' Association, as he was also head of the NHLPA. While in town, he would take his clients out for dinner. I was at his dinner in Vancouver when one of his assistants came over and asked me what my name was. And then I saw him go right over to Al to tell him.

I never needed to tell Bill who I was. Bill left Sports Management Ltd. around the time I was traded, and I went with him. Without Bill and his staff, Joyce and I would have been lost in Toronto. We were two young kids, twenty-one and twenty-two years old, in a big city. The traffic was so overwhelming, it used to leave Joyce in tears. Bill and his staff did a lot for us. They helped us find a house in the suburbs, and the accountant had us on a budget and handled the financial things we knew nothing about: taxes, mortgage payments, leases on the cars. They sent me to a clothiers to get decent suits, showed us around the city. And we had frequent dinners at Bill's house with him and his wife, Naddy. I wasn't eager to leave him and become a forgettable member of Alan Eagleson's stable. Eagleson didn't like to take no for an answer, though. He'd soon try a different approach.

After the record-setting season, over the summer and heading into training camp, I got the vibe that people expected me to hit 50 again in 1982–83. The fact that we were coming off one of the worst records in modern franchise history and had traded away some of our best players didn't seem to factor into that expectation, but no matter. I didn't feel any pressure to do it again. I wanted to, though. I had a good centreman in Billy Derlago, I was young, I was in good shape and healthy. Why not?

Know this: 50 is a big number. In any league, it is still a benchmark, a target and a bragging point. Rocket Richard was the first to get there; he did it in 1944–45, in 50 games. Then Bernie "Boom Boom" Geoffrion scored 50 with the Habs in 64 games in 1961. Bobby Hull did it four times in a row in Chicago, raising the bar to 58 in 1969. Phil Esposito took it up to 76 goals in 1971 with

Boston, and then Wayne Gretzky took it into the stratosphere in Edmonton, with 92 the same year I got my 54, so I was somewhat overshadowed. Gretzky, who also had an 87-goal season, scored 50 or more goals nine times, but Mike Bossy did it in a record nine consecutive seasons. Of course, Gretz also scored 50 in 39 games—by far the fastest—in 1981–82. A total of 91 players have scored 50 or more goals in a season. It's tough to score 50 goals, regardless of the style of hockey that is being played. Back in the eighties, there was more scoring than there is today, but it was also a different game because there was so much hooking, holding, obstruction, and cross-checking from defencemen in front of the net. There are enough equalizers between the decades to say 50 is still a magical number, and because I hadn't been trying to hit it in 1981–82, I don't think I appreciated just how hard it is to do.

The 1982–83 season started slowly for me. I had quit smoking again that summer, and for whatever reason I didn't score my first goal until the fifth game—a rare short-handed goal (I didn't kill many penalties)—and I had just one through 15 games. I started smoking again around that time, and my wife gave me some advice: Get out there and drop the gloves, Joyce told me. Get engaged, get your fire going. Bill Watters said the same thing. So I did. I can't remember who I fought, but I guess he was my lucky charm. I'd had only five goals in 20 games, but I got to 24 by the midway point of the season. I was heating up. By the sixtieth game I had 42, and I was at 48 by the seventy-first. Four games later, I had 49. It took me three more games, but number 50 arrived on March 30, 1983, at Joe Louis Arena in Detroit, a 4–2 win. It was a one-timer off the faceoff. Billy took the draw, won it right back to me, and I popped it top shelf, short side on Gilles Gilbert at 11:35 of the third period.

It's funny. The first time I scored 50 it was memorable and exciting. The second time just wasn't the same. It was just another moment. I mean, it's a big moment, but we still weren't a very good team—we finished that season with 68 points—and that took a little bit of the shine off. It was frustrating. I scored the fifty-first in the final game of the season, a 4–3 win in Buffalo. We made the playoffs despite ourselves that season, but lost 3–1 in the opening round to Minnesota.

And then there was Harold. That was my fourth year with the Leafs, and when it looked like I was going to get 50 again, the press asked Harold about my contract. It was up at the end of the year, and the media were suggesting Harold was going to have to pay me pretty well, the way the goals were piling up. I wasn't looking forward to the process.

You could argue that Harold didn't take running the business as seriously as he took saving it money. TC Puck was Harold's dog. He was in all our team pictures and always running around the arena. One year, I think it might have been this one, we were all posed in rows for the team photo. It was taking a long time for the photographer to get set up. I'm the captain, sitting near the middle in the front row. Harold is beside me, and the dog was at his feet on the ice. When we were finally done, the dog tried to get up but immediately started yelping. His balls were stuck to the ice. They had to call the dog walker to gently get him off the ice (don't ask me how, exactly, they did that, but the next year Harold's girlfriend, Yolanda, solved the problem—she tucked a towel underneath the dog). That was the stuff that drove me, and everybody else, crazy. His bloody dog in a team picture.

Another one: One summer I was working at former Ranger Walt Tkaczuk's hockey camp near Kitchener, Ontario. Joyce was pregnant at the time, and I remember her getting angry one day and saying she was done with Harold. Turns out he'd gone on a CBC Radio show and more or less told host Barbara Frum that women should be barefoot and pregnant and kept in the kitchen. She told Walt about it and he said, "That would never happen with the Rangers." But it happened with Harold. For years he ignored the league and wouldn't let female sportswriters into the dressing room. He was quoted as saying something to the effect that the best place for a woman is flat on her back.

He used to say some stupid stuff about his players, too. Laurie Boschman, who I lived with my first year after the trade, had become a born-again Christian. Harold called Bosch a Bible-thumper in the media. He was later traded. He once said in the newspapers of Inge Hammarström, who had come over from Sweden with Börje, that he could "go into a corner with six eggs in his pockets and not break any of them." That was Harold. Any time things were normal or quiet, he would make noise and headlines.

So you can imagine what it would be like to ask that type of guy for a raise.

When the reporters asked him about my contract, Harold replied that I would have been an ordinary player in the six-team league. "I'm not going to give him another dime," he said.

That's why players have agents. And I still had mine. Alan Eagleson had tried again. In 1983, Joyce and Lee Palmateer (our goalie Mike's wife—Mike was an Eagleson client) went to West Palm, Florida, for a vacation. They were staying at a condo owned by Eagleson, and he took them out for a champagne brunch. Lee was singing his praises, and he tried to talk Joyce into convincing me to hire him. It wasn't as flashy as the steak dinner in Toronto, but he was too clever to try something twice if it didn't work the first time. Unfortunately for him, the approach backfired. Joyce found him loud and rude, and she couldn't stand the way he was hounding us. So that pretty much sealed it: I was staying with Bill Watters.

Well, Harold did give me another dime—a few more, actually. This time, Bill managed to get a three-year deal at around $180,000, $200,000 and $225,000. I thought it was pretty nice, going from $70,000 to $180,000. I certainly wasn't upset. With my numbers, I was due at least double what I had been making. And I got it.

I still believe players in Toronto were paid less than guys on other teams who were putting up similar numbers. Bossy came into the league two years before me and was making in the $600,000 range. And Börje Salming, on our team, was making more than I was. I think the negotiations went smoothly, and it got done relatively quietly and quickly. Remember, back then we didn't have free agency until we were thirty-one. We also didn't have salary disclosure, which would have helped a lot of us get more money.

Joyce and I lived in the same house in Don Mills for the seven years I was with the Leafs. We bought it in 1980 for $140,000. It wasn't a mansion, but it was a nice house. I don't think we did anything differently once I was making more. Fortunately for me, Joyce is careful with our money and we saved a bit, and we were still on that budget that Bill's accountant had come up with for us. I was the one who spent the damn money—I was the stupid one! What I really could have used was for someone to grab me by the collar when I was nineteen years old and say, "Listen, start putting some money away."

I was bad with cars. I would get one, and then a new model would come out the next year and I had to have it. I've lost track of how many cars I had over the years. It was a lot. The next thing you know, you're losing $10,000 to $20,000 every time you change cars. So that was pretty stupid.

When I got that new contract, naturally I bought a new car. Mostly I bought SUVs and pickup trucks, but this time I bought the Audi 5000 Turbo. That wasn't cheap.

I didn't do many endorsements. Titan sticks paid me a little. I switched to Daoust skates one year and they paid me $5,000, but I didn't like the skates and went back to Bauer the following year. I'd say the most I ever made in endorsements in a year was maybe $8,000, so not a lot. There were a few years when I did a thing for a dealership and was given a couple of cars.

In January, I played in my second of three consecutive all-star games, this one in New Jersey. As usual, the festivities were more memorable than the game. And as usual for the Leafs, they were memorable for the wrong reasons. Harold didn't like to go to the all-star game or pay for the Leafs to have a table at the gala dinner held the night before. But Anne Murray was singing as part of the evening's entertainment (she sang at a few all-star games), and Joyce and I didn't want to miss her—table or not. Anne had season tickets at the Gardens and, I think, a soft spot for me because I was a fellow Maritimer (she's from Springhill, Nova Scotia). We were once both invited to Wayne Gretzky's charity tennis tournament in his hometown of Brantford, Ontario, and I heard she agreed to play only if we were paired together. We were, and we had a blast.

When Joyce and I got to the dinner, the Chicago executives let us sit with them. Bill Wirtz was chairman of the NHL Board of Governors, so maybe it was a league executives' table. It didn't matter. It was embarrassing to sit at the table of another team's owner, so we didn't stay long. Too bad, because during her set, Anne asked if I would join her on stage for a song, and I missed it.

Anne knew I liked to sing because she was part of a circle of friends I'd made in Toronto who had a way of showing up in interesting places. Anne was one. John Allan Cameron, a folksinger from down east, was another. But there was nobody quite like the comic actor John Candy. One year, Joyce and I hosted the team Halloween party, and we invited John and his wife, Rose. John took us to the costume storage for *SCTV* to get costumes and makeup so nobody would recognize us when we arrived. It was a barn dance at a place we'd found in the country, complete with a live band. Billy Harris, a big winger playing with us then, booked a stretch limo and brought a bunch of the guys out. The limo somehow got filled with straw during the night. The driver was not impressed. I sang that night. Jeff Brubaker did, too. He had an awesome voice. Börje was dancing up a storm. John and Rose had a fun time.

John was great, but he could be a handful. One night, when Rose wasn't with him, he joined us at Mr. Greenjeans, the players' favourite downtown haunt. He was putting away two double rum and

Cokes at a time, and growing more demanding with the waitress as the evening went on. It wasn't good. Everyone there knew who I was, so after that night we had to stop going. John would get even more involved in the Toronto sports scene a few years later, in 1991, when he bought the Canadian Football League's Toronto Argonauts, along with Wayne Gretzky and Bruce McNall. Sadly, he died of a heart attack in 1994.

Anne had also taken a turn at trying to own a Toronto sports franchise: the Leafs. In 1983 she was part of the team behind a $40 million offer to buy us away from Harold. That would have been fantastic. Deep down we kind of knew he'd never sell—he was making too much goddamned money. But we were still hoping. He said he wanted $100 million. That was that.

In 1983–84, I scored 52 goals—which made it 50-plus for three consecutive seasons. This time, though, the elation of the previous seasons was replaced with an empty feeling. In the seventy-second game, on March 14, I scored two goals in a 3–3 tie (yes, there were ties back then) against Minnesota and goaltender Gilles Meloche to hit 50, and then scored two more against Chicago down the stretch to finish with 52. That season I had 93 points, my career best.

You can't not be happy with scoring 50 goals, but when you don't make the playoffs it's not fun, and that year we missed again, finishing with 61 points. Brutal. You come to the rink every day and it's miserable when you're losing, knowing your season is going to come to a hard stop.

Hockey becomes a job. I hate to put it that way, but that's exactly what happens. It becomes a chore to play, not like when you're winning and having fun. When you play a sport for a living, it is a job, but there still should be some joy in it. That's part of what drives you. You have to work hard, but you should still be able to enjoy yourself on the ice, at practice, around the room, on the planes—or, in my case, maybe not on the planes.

I mentioned earlier that I hate flying. Always have, always will. It's a control thing. I like to be in control. I'm not a great passenger in a car either. If someone else's foot is on the gas pedal and brake, I feel like I'm putting my life in their hands. Then there are the variables that come with flying: weather conditions, human error, mechanical error. I just don't like it. And five seasons into my NHL career, I'd spent a lot of time in planes.

Wayne Gretzky hated flying, too. He once said it took a lot out of him. Just think what he could have done otherwise! Looking back on those three 50-goal seasons—how they came early in my career and on teams that weren't winning—I know my fear of flying certainly didn't help my career. Imagine sitting on a plane for two or three hours, maybe longer, and basically holding on to the arms of your seat with white knuckles, nervous and tense the entire time. Mentally and physically, it feels almost like playing an extra game. You're exerting so much energy, and sustaining so much tension, that you're emotionally drained by the time your feet are back on solid ground.

Road trips were terrible. The night before, I'd worry about flying. Every single time. I wouldn't sleep very much—and I was already a poor sleeper because of my bladder problem—and then I would think about getting on that plane the whole next day. The flight crews would often let me sit in the jump seat with the pilots for takeoff and landing, and that helped a little. But when I came out of the cockpit, my shirt would be drenched in nervous sweat. It was exhausting.

I had my coping strategies. At most NHL rinks, a few older gentlemen are assigned to the visitors' dressing room, and they help out the trainers with the equipment, loading the truck, unpacking the gear, that sort of stuff. Those guys always had beer stashed away. We had those gentlemen in Toronto, too, and they'd help me out. I would flip them a few bucks and they'd stash a six-pack in my bag. That took a little of the edge off and helped me get on the plane. It was the only way I could cope with all the flying. But even if I drank four of those six beers, or maybe even all six, it still didn't make the anxiety go away. I'd probably need ten to forget I was on a plane. Being drunk on a team charter cost me a $500 fine once. The team kept it quiet, but my self-medicating was noticed—and not appreciated.

In my rookie season, in Vancouver, they would always have one of those plastic garbage bins full of ice and beer after home games. We didn't have that at home in Toronto, but on the road there would always be a couple of two-fours of beer in the room. That helped get me on planes, but it couldn't have helped my game.

The Leafs chartered turboprops, those little old Air Ontario Convair 580s and 640s. Vancouver used them, too, when we were on eastern road trips. We'd fly to Toronto, make it our hub, and fly Convairs to wherever we were going (Buffalo did the same thing when I played there). The thing about those little planes? They couldn't rise above a storm. If there was crappy weather on the horizon, you knew it was going to be a rough flight. That wasn't easy. One time we went from Boston to St. Louis, which normally takes maybe three hours, and it took almost five because of head-winds. I was wiped out by the time we got there. On the best of days, the post-flight fatigue was a problem, because with the Leafs, when we were leaving Toronto, we never departed for anywhere until 7:35 p.m., which meant we'd arrive stupidly late, wherever we were going. But that way Harold didn't have to pay our meal money. And any travel for team business after 3 p.m. meant he was only obligated to pay a half-day per diem.

When I'd step on one of those Convairs, all I could think was that I loved my wife and hoped someday to see my kids grow up. I understood the statistics, but I didn't want to be the guy on the wrong side of them. I understood how many flights there were every day and every year, and how many safe landings—people would keep telling me that, trying to be reassuring. One person who understood me was Rick Fraser, one of the newspaper beat writers covering the team. He was a wonderful guy, a great and fair reporter, and a nervous flyer (who sadly has left us, but not because of a plane crash!). I'd see how nervous Ricky was on flights, when we all flew commercial. (Harold wouldn't let the media on the charters.) Anyway, Ricky's favourite drink was Canadian Club rye and water. On the road, he would keep a bottle of CC in his carry-on, and when he got on the plane, the first thing he'd do was ask the flight attendant for a glass of ice water. One time, it was early in the morning, but Ricky still asked for his glass of ice water.

The attendant smiled and said, "Now, I don't want to see that water change colour."

Ricky said, "Then don't look!"

Ricky used to say, "I'm tired of people telling me if your number is up, your number is up; there's nothing you can do about it." He'd say, "Okay, if my number's up that's fine, but what about the guy across the aisle? What if his number is up? How do I fit into that equation?" And then he'd drink his CC. I liked Ricky's logic.

Flying wasn't fun, and for a number of years it fit right in with everything else around the team. We just weren't enjoying the game. For all three of those years that I hit the 50 mark, it was almost like if our line didn't score we had no chance of winning the game. Billy and Danny Daoust and Tom Fergus, the three centres I played with over those years—I had great chemistry with all of them. But a lot of nights it felt like we were on our own. And I hated losing more than I liked winning. That's the way I was as a kid; I didn't like losing at anything.

To put those seasons in historical perspective, a number of Leafs had gotten close to 50 in years past: Frank Mahovlich had his 48 goals, and then Lanny McDonald had seasons with 46, 47 and 43; Darryl had 45 one year. And then Gary Leeman scored 51 during the 1989–90 season. Dave Andreychuk became the third Leaf to do it, in 1992–93, although there's an asterisk of sorts next to that one because he scored 29 of the goals with Buffalo, and then 25 with the Leafs over 83 games. The next season, he scored 53, all of them with the Leafs. So, just the three of us. So far.

John Tavares, the current Leafs captain, had 47 in Toronto in 2018–19, and Auston Matthews had 47 and counting in 70 games, on pace for 55, when the 2019–20 season was paused by the

COVID-19 virus. I was convinced Auston was going to score at least 50. He had a dozen games to get there and beyond, to hit 50 . . . or 55! And it would have been great if he did both.

Auston has unbelievable talent and vision, and a great shot. He can pick top corners with his snap shot, something a lot of guys can't do. He makes great passes and has an uncanny knack for finding people open. He's a big, strong guy. He has put up darn good numbers since he came into the league, scoring more than 30 goals every year—40, 34, 37, 47—and in those two seasons with 30-plus goals, he missed games with injuries. He's had four very strong years. I'll be shocked if he doesn't score 50 or more in a coming season.

Not long ago, I was talking with Auston at a Leafs gala. I told him, "I hope you get 55." I said it would be great if he did it, because at least I could say a guy who is a helluva goal scorer and player, and not some chump who got lucky, broke my record. I heard someone on a radio show saying there's no way Rick Vaive is hoping Auston's going to break his record. Not true. I'd be very happy for him, because I know how hard it is to do. And I'd be the first to congratulate him, like Frank Mahovlich did for me.

But even more than scoring 50, I hope for Auston's sake that he's able to win a Stanley Cup. That's your goal when you come into the league. You might think of scoring 50 only in your wildest dreams, but everyone who steps on NHL ice dreams of winning the Cup.

I don't have very many regrets in life, but never getting to hoist the Stanley Cup is one of them. I'd give up two of those

50-goal seasons—not the first one, but the other two—for an NHL championship. Imagine being the captain of the Toronto Maple Leafs and winning the Stanley Cup!

We weren't dreaming of too many Cups in Toronto back then, but the next season brought us what we thought might be the missing ingredient—the guy who would help make us a competitive team.

8

THE KID FROM KELVINGTON

At the start of the 1984–85 season, I read somewhere that the odds-makers had set the chances of the Maple Leafs winning the Stanley Cup at—wait for it—4,000 to 1.

I wouldn't have taken that action with *your* money! And the oddsmakers weren't wrong.

Hockey season got off to a rough start for me. Team Canada beat the Swedes for the Canada Cup in September, but I hadn't made the team. I played a few exhibition games, though, including one against the US in Montreal. Near the end of the game I got into a scuffle with Chris Nilan, the scrappy winger from Boston who was playing with the Canadiens at the time. There was some slashing. It wasn't really a fight. There were only a couple of minutes left in the game, so we both got kicked out. The next day, after practice, Brian Sutter and I were standing in the lobby of the Forum, waiting for the team bus. Nilan was walking by on his way to practice and started yapping at me. Then he turns and slaps me in the face with an open hand. Some people said he slugged me, but it was a slap. Brian O'Neill, who was an executive vice-president with the NHL, investigated what happened. There was talk about charges being laid. The authorities interviewed me, and apparently Chris as well. I had no intention of pressing any charges, that's for sure. Later, during the season, when the Leafs were in Montreal practising, I was standing by the bench, drinking water, and Chris came and sat on the bench and said he was sorry for what happened. We both moved on.

I got an unexpected vote of confidence after I was cut from Team Canada, though. Not long after the roster was announced, we got a call at home. It was Gunner, the Leafs' trainer, and he had Harold on the line. I thought that was pretty cool, Harold calling me at home. It was the first time he'd ever reached out to me. He said he was pissed off that I didn't make the team, that it was a mistake, that they didn't know their asses from a hole in the ground. I don't know whether he was pissed off for me, or pissed off because a Leaf didn't make the team. I still wonder if he was so mad because it was Alan Eagleson running the Canada Cup, and Harold hated him. Anyway, Harold wouldn't be calling me at home again that season. And it was going to be a long one.

Mike Nykoluk had been fired as our head coach during the off-season. I had my three best pro seasons under Mike, who treated me and all the other players with respect. Was he a great coach? No. But he got the best out of some of us. Mike was totally different from the other guys we'd had behind the bench. He never raised his voice. He would often call me into his office and we would talk, but not always about hockey. He was a very nice man. Maybe too nice, too easy on the guys. Some of them were going out at night, not producing, not going as hard as they could, knowing that Mike wasn't going to come down on them. But I enjoyed playing for Mike; he just let me play.

Dan Maloney, who was the assistant coach and a former teammate of mine, took over from Mike. We knew he was going to be a hard-ass, and we really weren't very happy. It wasn't going to be pleasant and we knew it. No surprise, he'd eventually pick fights with his best players.

That season, we won our first two games in overtime, so not a bad start. But by the end of the calendar year, we'd won a grand total of six games. We were 6-30-5 when we won our seventh game. Dan was losing his mind. We finished that season 20-52-8—a whopping 48 points, the worst in franchise history in the modern era—dead last in the NHL. A .300 win percentage. Our goals for were 253, dead last. Our goals against were 358, third last.

We were horrible that season, and it seemed we were at our worst at home. The fans let us know it, too: sweaters thrown on the ice, bags on their heads. It weighed on us. One day partway through the season, I got frustrated. A few hours earlier, I'd gone for my nap and had asked Joyce to wake me up early. I wanted to get to the rink early. But she let me sleep about an hour longer than I'd wanted. I was mad when I woke up and saw the time. I got dressed and was about to leave for the rink, but when I opened the door, the dog—we had a German shepherd puppy named Assenta—ran outside. I'm in my suit and dress shoes chasing after the dog, and the dog thinks we're playing a game. I couldn't get it to come in. So I slammed the screen door and the glass shattered. Next thing I know, the dog is at the door. I grab her to keep her away from the glass and throw her into the backyard. I was yelling and screaming at Joyce. I just lost it. It took her an hour to get the dog back inside, it was so scared. When I got to the rink I called Joyce and apologized. But we were on edge. It wasn't fun that season, and it's pretty shitty when the fans are booing you at home. It was frustrating. The team was going on the road after that meltdown, and I was looking forward to it.

After three straight 50-goal seasons, I scored 35. People asked what had happened. I fell short, simply put. Our power play, like everything else, wasn't very good, certainly not as good as the previous seasons. With the team we had, 35 goals wasn't a bad year. But you go from 52 goals to 35 and everyone notices. It only figured that everyone's numbers were going to go down, and they did. All things considered, I thought 35 was still pretty good.

I was having neck problems at the time as well. It seemed like every time I got hit I had a burning feeling down my arm, like I'd stuck my hand in an oven. It would go away after five or six minutes, so I'd go back out, get hit again and I'd have the same awful feeling. A little numbness remained, and that made it hard to shoot. I was never much of a stickhandler, so that wasn't much of a problem. We all had injuries. We'd play the whole year with injuries, especially back when you didn't have a sports science team that would tell you to sit out for however long was needed to get healthy. But those stingers in my neck and arm sure didn't help.

We had good doctors, but our medical trainer, Guy Kinnear, was Harold's boat mechanic in Midland, Ontario, where Harold had his cottage during the off-season. I'm sure Gunner took some courses, but he was by no means qualified for the job. I'd heard he fainted when he saw blood. John Anderson used to say, "If we had boats we know where to take them!" That season, I missed eight games with injuries and played hurt in a ton more. I don't know how many charley horses I had during my time in Toronto. A few years later, when I got to Chicago, I had a charley horse and the trainer gave me a wrap, told me to bend the leg, sleep like that, and I would be good to practise the next day. It worked. In Toronto, we didn't have a trainer who could get us back that quickly. And they always figured you were ready to play when you weren't. So you play, and obviously you don't play as well as you can if you are healthy. It wasn't just the Leafs; not many teams had certified trainers back then.

Every day we had to wait for Gunner to finish Harold's legs, but even then he could only do so much for you. One morning after a game, I went into his room and said, "I don't know what I did last night, Gunner, but my shoulder is aching." So he goes into his bag and he hands me two packs of NeoCitran. I said, "What the fuck is that for?" He tells me I must be getting the flu because I said my shoulder was aching. I said, "Okay, let me rephrase that. My shoulder hurts." He said, "That'll help." I said, "Okay, whatever." We called Gunner and Danny Lemelin, our equipment manager, the Hiding Brothers, because you could never find them when you needed something. Danny—or Smokey, as we called him—had a room down the hall behind the bench. I remember going to his door to get my skates sharpened. I could see light under the door, but it was locked. I was banging, but he wouldn't answer. He was having a smoke break, so I had to jump on the ice with dull blades.

By the end of the season, Harold was being quoted in the newspapers saying the Leafs should trade me and Anderson. Every year I was in Toronto, except for my first, I scored 30 or more goals. Maybe he was disappointed with 35. Who knows. It wasn't surprising he would say something like that; he was always trying to make headlines. To be honest, there were times that summer when I was hoping, at least in the back of my mind, I would get traded. But I didn't have any control over where I would end up, and half of the twenty-one teams were lousy.

It was a Catch 22 situation. Again. For the team: to get better, you need more talent, but to get talent, you have to trade talent away. For me: to not waste my career, I could leave Toronto, but I could land with a team that was bad and trading away its future to get an established scorer. Be careful what you wish for! It was possible that I'd end up in a situation that was somehow even worse than the one I was in, although that was hard to imagine. Damned if you, damned if you don't. And deep down, as much as that was the worst of all my seasons with the Leafs, I didn't want to leave Toronto.

My grandmother was a wise and generous woman, and she used to tell me that if you look hard enough you can find a silver lining, no matter how bad it might seem. Being the worst team in the NHL could have an upside. In this case, it did—because it meant we had the first overall pick in the 1985 draft. Of course, we already had a lot of top draft picks: Craig Muni, Bob McGill, Fred Boimistruck, Jim Benning, Gary Nylund, Gary Leeman, Peter Ihnačák, Ken Wregget, Russ Courtnall, Al Iafrate, Todd Gill—but we rushed them all, put them in the NHL before they were ready, and it made it really difficult for them. They needed time to learn how to be a pro. Almost all of them eventually did have good careers, but it was tough sledding for a while for them and us.

Here is how bad things had become in Toronto: Prior to the 1984 draft, a kid named Craig Redmond, who was a defenceman from British Columbia playing for Team Canada, reportedly sent a letter to a few teams—the Leafs being one of them—saying he wouldn't play for those teams if one of them drafted him. I'm surprised a kid would say that. I just can't imagine doing it. Maybe as a free agent you pick your spots, but certainly not in the draft. Maybe he thought he couldn't handle the pressure in Toronto, or maybe he didn't want to be part of the circus with Harold—but Harold was getting to an age where he wasn't going to be around much longer anyway. Turns out it was in 1990 that he died, but he was out of the picture before then. If I'd been in that kid's shoes, I would have looked at getting drafted by the Leafs as a situation in which I could be part of the solution. Anyway, the Leafs took a pass on Redmond and chose Iafrate with the fourth overall pick, which was ultimately the far better choice. Alfie had a good career, and Redmond, drafted sixth overall by Los Angeles, played just 191 games in the NHL.

In 1985, scouts from around the league were looking seriously at Craig Simpson—a talented winger from London, Ontario, playing at Michigan State—as the best player in the draft. There were reports that Craig and his family met with Leafs GM Gerry McNamara and Maloney and the meeting did not go well, to the point that Craig didn't want to be drafted by Toronto, although later reports suggested that a second meeting repaired the damage.

We were also hearing that if we didn't select Simpson first overall, the Leafs would take Dana Murzyn, a six-foot-two, 200-pound defenceman playing junior in Calgary. Well, the Leafs did pick a defenceman from the west, but his name was Wendel Clark. And I can't imagine any fan ever wishing the team had selected someone else. Simpson went second to Pittsburgh and Murzyn dropped to number five, taken by Calgary. Craig Wolanin was selected third by New Jersey, and Jim Sandlak was taken fourth by Vancouver.

As a player on a terrible team, you pay attention to the draft. Over the course of the season and leading up to the draft, the names would come out in the media. We'd watch the world junior tournament to see some of the top prospects. Wendel was a defenceman in the Western Hockey League with the Saskatoon Blades. But the only way he could make the Canadian world junior team was if he played forward. They also told him he had to cut his hair, which he did!

I watched a little bit of the tournament. They were talking about him potentially being the number-one pick overall, and I thought he'd be a helluva a guy to get on our team, especially knowing that in order to make that team he'd had to move to left wing. He was so composed. He played hard, wasn't afraid to bang guys. He had that tremendous wrist shot. After finishing dead last, once you got past the sting of it, the draft was something to look forward to, knowing we were going to be adding another good young player. Of course, in the back of my mind I'm wondering if they're going to fuck it up.

Because we had rushed so many good picks, it almost didn't matter who we were getting unless the guy was physically and mentally ready to play in the NHL, and it had to be both. We knew they would put the guy in the lineup right away. But we got lucky with Wendel; he was ready both physically and mentally. Wendel was committed to playing hard every night, and he came in leading by example. As a kid, playing the way he did… that really helped our team, because guys would look at what he was doing and have no choice but to follow. He made an impression from the first day of training camp.

First and foremost, Wendel is a great guy. He's a farm boy. He's not cocky; he's not arrogant; he was happy to be playing in the NHL. He gave us 100 percent. Those guys are hard to find—the full package of a guy who could score goals, play physical, fight the toughest opponents, and every night give everything he had. If you're picking number one overall, that's the kind of player you want to have.

I was at the draft, which was held at the Metro Convention Centre in Toronto. It was the first time the draft was held outside Montreal. The previous five years it had been at the Forum, and the league now expected to be able to use Maple Leaf Gardens. They underestimated Harold. Ballard didn't like league president John Ziegler, and he didn't like the league telling him what to do. So Harold scheduled a big maintenance project, ripping up the Gardens floor, to coincide with the draft. Typical Harold.

I sat at the Leafs table along with Harold, John Brophy (who spent a couple of years as Dan Maloney's assistant), the scouts and some of the front office. They weren't looking for my draft advice. My job as captain was to meet the kids, welcome them to the team. I was happy to do it. After Wendel was selected, we talked for a bit.

I told him the usual stuff: it was nice to have him with the club, do what you do, do it to the best of your ability and you'll be fine, don't worry about any of the crap. I don't think the expectations of him were really high, even though he was the first overall pick. I knew they were planning to play him on the wing and that would be an adjustment, even though he'd done it at the world juniors. I was a little worried, because I knew he was tough and liked to fight. He wasn't very big, yet he'd still fight anyone, any size. Of course, fighting Wendel usually ended up being the other guys' problem. I told him, don't worry about the fans, the coaches, management and the owner; you'll be fine. Even though he was coming from a small farm town—Kelvington, Saskatchewan—I got the sense pretty quickly that he wouldn't have trouble adjusting to life in Toronto. He just seemed like he had things under control.

After such a horrible season, getting Wendel first overall— even though we didn't know how good he would be—gave us a sense of hope. It was there for me. I thought we had some good young players, but you add Wendel, you look at the big picture— perhaps in two or three years we're going to have a pretty darn good team.

Wendel had a terrific rookie season, scoring 34 goals and earning 227 penalty minutes—tough as nails, a hard hitter, fun to watch. He was a great addition. And we played him on left wing. It didn't surprise me, the seamless transition he made from defence to for- ward, and he was great: he had 37 goals the next season, 1986–87. As good as he was on the wing, I would have liked to see him on defence. He still would have been a big hitter, tough around our net, and he would have gotten some space on the ice to carry the puck and create some offence. He might have really solidified our blue line. He could have been a terrific defenceman in that era.

Wendel was one of the first teammates to shoe-check me. We were at a team meal, I don't remember exactly when or where, when he slid under the table and lathered ketchup or sour cream or something all over my shoes. I always dressed nicely when the team was out on the town and had on a fantastic pair of suede shoes. Wendel appears suddenly in his seat, after crawling back under the table, and yells, "Shoe check!" My shoes were done. I was pretty mad about those shoes, but that's just life with the team.

With Wendel and his wicked snap shot, and me with my big slapshot, we had a lethal combination up front, on the left and right side—two guys who could score, play physical. And we had some good talent around us. We just didn't have a lot of secondary scoring, and our goaltending still wasn't the best. We picked up Don Edwards, who'd played some good years in Buffalo, but that didn't work out well. We also had Ken Wregget and Tim Bernhardt, and Allan Bester played one game. Donny was pretty much at the end of his career, and he struggled with us. Timmy was okay. Wregget would eventually get better, but at the time they were basically Band-Aids that didn't work, and it didn't help that overall, defensively, we didn't have any direction.

For NHL teams, losing means high draft picks. But for many players, watching your team acquire talented young players who might one day make you better but also might take your job is cold comfort. For top players from each country, a more enjoyable result of a season without playoffs is, if you're lucky enough to receive it, an invitation to join your country's team at the World

Championships. At the end of that dismal 1984–85 season, before attending the draft that would land Wendel, I was invited to play for Team Canada in Prague. It was actually my second appearance at the tournament. I had gone to the Worlds in Helsinki in 1982.

I remember Helsinki especially well, because we had a heckuva team in '82. Edmonton had been upset in the first round of the playoffs by the Los Angeles Kings—remember the Miracle on Manchester?—so we had Wayne Gretzky and a few other Oilers, a few Montreal Canadiens (Bob Gainey), Philadelphia Flyers (Bobby Clarke, Bill Barber), Mike Gartner and Dale Hawerchuk. We had a good defence, guys like Craig Hartsburg and John Van Boxmeer. Darryl Sittler was there, too.

There were eight teams in our group, and we played a round robin against the other seven teams. Then the four best teams had another round robin. There was no actual medal round, which was a bit unlike other tournaments I'd played in. We finished the first round robin 3-2-2 and in fourth place, behind the unbeaten Soviets, Czechoslovakia and Sweden. We had beaten Finland, West Germany and the US; lost to the Czechs and Soviets; tied Sweden and Italy.

In the second round, we lost to the Soviets, then beat the Czechs and Swedes. The Czechs and Soviets were playing after our 6–0 win over Sweden. If the Soviets won, we would have won the silver, but they tied 0–0, which gave the Czechs the silver. It was a little bit of a heartbreak having to settle for bronze.

One game, they put me on a line with Gretzky. Playing with Wayne wasn't like playing with any other centre; it was better. His whole style of play was different from any centre I'd ever had. I was used to coming up the wing late on the rush and getting fed the puck as I crossed the blue line. But Gretz was so crafty, he would often make an extra move and I'd go offside. I didn't get a chance to adapt. After that game they took me off his line. One game, see you later. It would have been nice to have played a little longer with Gretz, because I would have figured out what he liked to do. I would have come a little later, or gone to the other side of the ice and got lost so the D would forget about me for a second or two—he'd have found me before they did.

Helsinki was still a great experience, and I wound up with three goals and an assist in nine games.

In 1985, still stinging from not playing in the Canada Cup the previous fall, I got a measure of redemption. Gretz wasn't available, but nineteen-year-old Mario Lemieux was. I remember he wanted to leave the team and go home at one point. Maybe he was homesick, being so young and having just finished a 100-point rookie NHL season. Several players and management had to talk him into staying, and thankfully he did. Even at that age, he led us in scoring.

We had four top centres in Mario, Steve Yzerman, Ron Francis and my linemate in the tournament, Bernie Nicholls. Bernie had just come off a 100-point season himself, in LA. I was feeling at home on the team, because rounding out our line was John Anderson, my left wing in Toronto. Andy had his house up for sale in Etobicoke, on the Kingsway, expecting he wouldn't be back with the Leafs in the fall. He, Billy and I were like little boys together, always staying up late, having beers, talking about making the playoffs and winning a Cup together. Andy could never make the weigh-in at Leafs training camp—he had to go to a friend's sauna for hours. If he looked at a hamburger he'd put on three pounds. He sweat so much he'd be soaked just playing cards on the plane. Billy use to call him Furnace Face, because he'd be as red as a beet after every shift.

We got along fine with Bernie. I had no idea he didn't drink, because he was always the life of the party. The stuff he did, you wouldn't have expected he'd be so disciplined. After the pre-game meal, he would sneak into one of the guys' rooms, get in the bathtub, pull the curtains and hide. One afternoon, I was sitting on the can—next thing he comes flying through the curtains screaming. I almost had a heart attack.

We beat the Soviets 3–1 in the final round, the first time Canada had beaten them at the Worlds since 1969. I should point out that it was the first time the Soviets were playing without their great goaltender Vladislav Tretiak since—guess when?—1969. But that was a sweet win. We also beat the US in the final round, but lost to the Czechs 5–3 to leave us with the silver medal. I had eight points in 10 games, good for second on the team behind Mario, and led Canada in goals, with six. That was nice.

Lighting it up and winning silver in Prague, playing that last tournament with Andy—it was a nice end to a tough season. And adding Wendel in Toronto: maybe life with the Leafs was finally headed in the right direction.

Right?

9

THE BIG MISTAKE

As a friend once said, being the captain of the Toronto Maple Leafs is one of hockey's greatest honours, but also one of its biggest burdens.

In the 103-year history of the franchise, twenty-five men have worn the "C," but only eighteen since 1927, when the team became known as the Maple Leafs. Think about some of the players who wore the "C" before me: George Armstrong, Dave Keon, Darryl Sittler, Ted Kennedy, Syl Apps, Charlie Conacher, Red Horner, Hap Day. All of them members of the Hockey Hall of Fame. Almost all of them Stanley Cup champions. All great players.

Since that last Stanley Cup win in 1967, just ten players have worn the "C." To have my name on that list, to be named captain of the Maple Leafs, was a tremendous honour.

And to have that captaincy taken away was a huge embarrassment.

For too many of us, that badge of honour eventually became a scarlet letter. In the past half-century, Armstrong was really the only one who moved on gracefully. He, of course, was captain of that 1967 Stanley Cup–winning team. He retired as a Leaf and remained with the organization for years. After him it was Keon—maybe the greatest Leaf of all time—then Sittler, and then me. None of us had a happy ending as captain, or as Leafs. It was the same for the captains who followed us: their time as a Leaf didn't end well. Some were traded (Wendel Clark, Doug Gilmour, Dion Phaneuf), one left as a free agent (Mats Sundin) and one (Rob Ramage) was left unprotected in an expansion draft. The good news is that a lot of those broken fences were mended. Keon, Sittler, Wendel, Doug and I are all involved with the team today, proud to be part of the Leafs alumni, while Mats still visits and Dion recently did a job shadow with club president Brendan Shanahan.

I knew I was too young, just twenty-two, when I was named the twelfth captain in team history. I wasn't ready for it, and the room wasn't ready for me to have that authority. But I thought I had matured and grown into the role and earned the respect of my teammates during the four years I wore the "C." I was very proud to be the captain.

But I made a mistake and I paid dearly for it.

On the morning of Saturday, February 22, 1986, I slept in and missed a 7:15 a.m. practice. Not long after I woke up, I was no longer captain.

We had played in Calgary on Thursday—I had two goals and an assist in a 7–6 overtime win—and had travelled to Minneapolis the next day. Back then, pretty much all the teams stayed in the Marriott Hotel in Bloomington, which was a suburb of Minneapolis; it was right next to the Met Center, where the North Stars played. You literally walked out the back door of the hotel and across a parking lot, and you were at the arena. It was that close. But in the dead of winter that frozen walk felt like it took forever. The rink, as well as the baseball/football stadium next to it, is long gone now, replaced by the gigantic Mall of America.

That Friday night, the Quebec Nordiques were playing the North Stars. John Anderson had been traded to the Nordiques in the summer, and I met him after the game to catch up. Johnny Rotten, as we called him—not because of the punk singer, but to tease him about the food at his chain of hamburger joints—was traded for a pretty good defenceman, Brad Maxwell. We had also traded Billy Derlago, so two of my linemates during my 50-goal seasons, two of my best friends, were gone. Billy was traded after our first game of the season. Typical of Harold's Maple Leafs, Billy had signed a new contract that summer, and Harold had told him he would be a Leaf forever. Billy believed him and started to renovate his house. After our opening game, in Boston, Dan Maloney told him he was being traded to the Bruins for Tom Fergus, who ended up becoming my centre, although at the time I was playing with Dan Daoust.

I was still on the ice with some good players, but it hurt to lose two good friends. With Billy, I guess you could see a deal coming. He came to camp a little out of shape and they told him he had training camp to get ready for the season. He didn't put the work in. Billy could rub the coaches the wrong way. Once, he was coming back from an injury and Broph was making him walk up and down the escalator in the Gardens, up the down side and down the upside. And he would get Billy on the bike, trying to get him back in shape. One day Billy was on the bike, having a nice easy ride along with a coffee and a cigarette. Broph came into the room and said, "What the fuck are you doing? If you're not going to try you might as well go home." And Billy said, "Okay, I'll see you tomorrow." Got off the bike, got dressed and left. Billy was just like that—so good, so talented, but at times it was like he didn't give a shit. He did. But he was funny, he was witty. Sometimes it was too much fun and not enough of what a coach wants to see.

So I wasn't really surprised he was traded, just disappointed. At the same time, the game is a business and I had to understand that. I couldn't look at it as losing a friend; instead, we were gaining a player in Tom who might help us be a better team. I was traded three times myself. Telling myself they were just trying to improve the team never made it feel better at the time, but that's business, and business is a part of any professional athlete's life.

Anyway, I hadn't seen Andy since he was traded in August. So that night in Minny, we had what I called at the time a late-night bull session.

I can't remember why, but Maloney had scheduled a 7:15 a.m. practice on Saturday morning. We had an afternoon game against the North Stars on Sunday. Andy and I hooked up and I had a fair bit to drink, but I was in my room around one in the morning. Greg Terrion was my roommate, and he woke me up that morning. I sat up in bed and he asked me if I was okay. I said, "Yup, I'm good," but I was never a good morning person. Greg left to go to the rink, and I laid my head on the pillow and fell back to sleep. Next thing I know, there's a knock on the door. It was Maloney. He wasn't very happy, which I could understand. I met later on with Dan and Gerry McNamara, the general manager, and that's when they said they were going to take the "C" away. Gerry was quoted in the newspapers the next day saying "it was a painful decision" that was made by him, Ballard and Maloney. Gerry said, "To have our team captain miss an important practice—it was important because we spent Friday travelling here and didn't practise that day—just isn't acceptable."

He wasn't wrong about missing the practice. It was a mistake, something I shouldn't have done, but I still believe the punishment was more severe than it should have been or needed to be. If I was the coach and my captain, one of the best players on the team, slept in, I would have been pissed off, too. But I'd have told him: "Here's the deal—I told the press and the team that you were sick, that's why you weren't at practice, but don't let it happen again, because the next time I won't stick up for you. I've got your back now but don't ever let this fucking happen again." That's all Dan had to do. If he had done that, I think he would have gotten more out of me as a player. He also would have gotten a lot more respect from me, and I would have done anything for him.

Instead, we're in Minneapolis with a game the next day and I'm no longer the captain.

I have to take accountability for what happened. It was my fault, and I shouldn't have stayed out so late drinking the night before. But I hadn't seen John in a long time and the Leafs were nearing the end of another long, tough season. We had started at a blistering 3-13-3 pace and were in last place. Börje got hurt. I broke my hand before Christmas.

We played Sunday afternoon and lost 4–3. We were down 3–0 after the first period, and 4–0 early in the second. I scored a power-play goal to make it 4–2 and finished the game with six shots. Before the game, I apologized to the guys for what I had done. I was wrong, and I shouldn't have done it. But, I said, it was over with; let's put it behind us and move on. That's the way I tried to deal with it. It wasn't fun. But the guys were good. There wasn't a whole lot said. I told them I wasn't going to play any differently than I played before, that I was going to go out there every night and try to be the best player I could be. I think I did that. I didn't sulk. I did what I would normally do, whether I had a letter on my sweater or not. And I still went on to score 33 goals that season and 32 the next.

After the game, Maloney called an early curfew for Sunday night, which was overdoing it. A lot of the guys came in while Dan, who'd been drinking, was checking curfew himself. One of them was Russ Courtnall, who didn't get along with Dan at all. He was rooming with Brad Smith. Danny was hammered and tried to go after Russ. Smitty stepped in the way, to try to calm things down, and Danny carved Smitty's back with a fucking pen. I was in my room, sound asleep, and had no idea what had happened. It had been an exhausting few days.

Dan and I returned from Minny on an early flight the morning after the game to avoid the media. We took the airport shuttle together, and he didn't say a word the whole time. When the guys flew back later in the day, Terrion called and told me everything that had happened the night before—that while Danny was checking curfew, he was fighting with a bunch of guys in the hallway, yelling and screaming. He shouldn't have been checking curfew while he was shit-faced, especially with a temper like his.

If I'm looking for a silver lining in that whole weekend, it's that I actually learned some good lessons for later on, when I became a coach.

In some ways, looking back, I'm not surprised everything transpired the way it did that weekend. I should have been smarter, and Danny (who recently passed away) was drinking heavily himself. As soon as the news got out that I'd lost the "C," the media were asking whether it was the prelude to a trade. After all, they knew Dan and I had a history. The previous season, 1984–85, there were a few clashes between us. It was his first season as a head coach and my goal production had dropped, mostly because our power play wasn't as good as it had been and I had some nagging injuries. I'd had a ton of hip pointers—basically a bruise on the hip bone—from getting run into the boards, which were much lower back then and didn't give the way they do now. I had a lot of charley horses, too, and a stupid rash that popped up occasionally and made my skin hurt and itch like hell. But Dan wasn't happy with me, and there were trade rumours even then.

Before he retired as a player, I had Danny as a left winger for a while. I remember at practices, we would be doing skating drills and Billy and I would go at two-thirds speed because we didn't want Danny—Snow Shoes, as we used to call him—to get too far behind us and look bad. We'd finish up and Danny would say, "Way to work, boys, way to work," and we'd say, "Sure, way to go, Danny."

As a coach, he was the complete opposite of Mike Nykoluk. That's what happened every time the Leafs changed coaches: we'd go from one extreme to the other. We had Floyd Smith, who was quiet; then Joe Crozier, who was a yeller and screamer; then Nykoluk, who didn't say boo; then Maloney, who had been Mike's assistant. But you had a job to do, whoever the coach was. Deal with it.

Danny came in and right away at that first training camp—it was in Belleville—he lived up to our expectations. Back then, it was two weeks of twice-a-day practices before you played an exhibition game. That rink in Belleville had Olympic-size ice, and he'd skate the hell out of us. Then, for some bizarre reason, he thought it was a good idea to take the water off the benches. Try getting that one past the sports scientists today. It was a gruelling camp. I guess he wanted to set the tone right away that he was the boss.

The Gardens had lots of those steel tray holders that snack vendors used to carry pop around the stands. We even had one in the dressing room. One night Danny came in, took the tray and flung it, and it hit Al Iafrate. The drinks were dripping off him, off his helmet, all over him. Danny kept screaming and yelling, and Alfie just sat there. He had all this pop and water and Gatorade dripping off him. He sat there with a sad face and didn't say a word.

Another night, we got beat badly in Winnipeg. We flew home the next day, got in around two in the afternoon and had to go straight to the Gardens to watch the entire goddamn game tape. Danny would stop periodically to point things out. Then we had to put on our gear for an hour's bag skate. I didn't get home until 6:30 that night. But that was the type of intense individual Danny was. He played that way. He was a hot-headed guy.

He was particularly hard on the young guys. One time, Courtnall had gone to Gerry to complain about him. In practice a few days later, everyone was wearing the different-coloured sweaters for their lines and there was one guy wearing a red sweater—it was Russ. Danny blew the whistle, called us all in at centre ice, and yelled, "Courtnall, do you know why you're wearing the red sweater?" Russ could be a bit of a smartass, but this time he said he didn't know why. Danny said, "It's because that was the colour of my goddamn face when I found out you went to McNamara complaining about me yelling at you young guys." A lot of that shit went on.

After that, Danny couldn't give the young guys crap like he used to. But we knew Danny, and we knew he had to find a way to get out his frustrations. Sometimes a coach, knowing he can't come down too hard on his younger players without spooking them, will talk to his veterans. He'll tell them, "I might say some things about you guys in the papers, but don't worry about it. I can't say anything about the young guys, but I have to say *something* so they know I'm not happy with the way the team's playing." Dan didn't do that; he just carried on. Anyway, we had upcoming home and away games coming on consecutive nights and we lost both. Billy, John and I didn't get a goal in either game. The next day in the papers, the headlines read, "Maloney blames Derlago's line for both losses." I'm thinking, *No big deal*, but then I start reading the article. He did call us out; he said it was our fault.

At the end of practice, Danny calls us to centre ice and says, "Anderson, Vaive, Derlago, stay on the ice." Walt Poddubny was coming back from an injury, so he was forced to stay on with us.

Danny started making us skate. I'm thinking, *What the fuck is this?* I said, "I guess you've got to blame somebody." Next thing, he started chasing me around the ice. I said, "Fuck you," and, of course, the reporters are there between the benches, watching. And then Broph, who was the assistant coach, started chasing me. He's saying, "Squid, Squid, settle down," so I said "Fuck you" to him, too. I was so mad. I think Danny was just frustrated and took it out on us. But all he had to do was talk to me.

The next game, we were at home against Philadelphia. He benched our line for the first half of the first period, and then he started playing Billy. John and I sat on the bench for the entire game. I never got a shift. I remember—some nights, the Gardens could get quiet at times—someone in the stands behind the bench yelled out, "Hey, Rick, you're not very busy. Could you go get me a hot dog?" Everybody in the building could hear it. I wanted so badly to turn and say to him, "What do you want on it?" But I knew if I said anything, Danny would have punched me in the head.

That game, we were down by two goals with about a minute and a half left. I'm thinking, *Don't put me on the ice.* If he did, I was going to say, "Danny, do you want me to win it, or just tie it up?" That was the start of our butting heads.

Our relationship never got any better after that. If anything, it got worse. It was partly my fault, because I didn't like the way he was doing things. I tuned him out and just played my game. It all led up to me losing the "C," though. I don't know if he had it in for me, but I sure wasn't listening to him.

After I lost the "C," I tried hard not to let it affect my play. Anytime something like that happens—when you know you should have been a little smarter—it's obviously not a good feeling. But I was pissed. First of all, it was a severe punishment for sleeping in. Like I said, we could have sorted it out between us. That's all it takes. But Dan's first reaction was to go to Gerry, then Harold, and the next thing you know they're at my fucking hotel room door and that was it. He was probably hungover and pissed off himself.

Joyce wasn't very happy about my losing the captaincy, or the reason I'd lost it, but she supported me. That helped a lot. Even though I knew she was pissed off, she was smart enough to know I was feeling bad enough already, and piling on wasn't going to help. Also, she had bigger, more important things to worry about. Our first son, Jeffrey, was born a few months earlier in October. We got flowers, teddy bears and gifts from fans and from sponsors like Molson and Titan. We got a Roots baby outfit and a pair of Nike baby shoes, baby blue with a swoosh (we still have those). Jeff was her main focus, not that she wasn't concerned after I lost the "C." It was awkward for her, as my wife, to go back to the Gardens after that. One day you're the captain's wife and a new mother being fussed over. Then you're not.

Despite us having only 57 points (which was nine more than the previous season) and going 2-7-1 down the stretch, we made the playoffs. Detroit had just 40 points, so we finished fourth in the Norris Division. And then something clicked. Chicago had finished first in the division with 29 more points than us, so we weren't supposed to have a chance. But we swept them in three games, winning 5–3 and 6–4 in Chicago, and 7–2 back home. Bob McGill was a big factor in that series because he bugged the hell out of Al Secord, who played on their big line. Bob fought him and got him off his game. That kind of rattled them as a team. I don't think a lot of the season ticket holders in Toronto had picked up their playoff tickets because we had been so bad. So Game 3 at the Gardens was full of fans who didn't normally have a chance to buy tickets, and the atmosphere was incredible. By the end of the game, they were throwing brooms on the ice; the noise was crazy. The building was alive and we won.

Funny story about Bob and Chicago. One Saturday night, we played at the Gardens and then chartered right after the game to Chicago to play the Blackhawks the next night. It was late when we got in, and Bob fell asleep on the team bus to the hotel. Someone said to leave him be. We got off the bus quietly and left him snoozing while the driver took the bus back to park for the night in a fenced-in lot in some terrible part of town. The attendant was getting ready to close the gate and lock up when Bobby woke up and started screaming at the guy not to leave him behind. He eventually got a cab to the hotel.

In the next round we met St. Louis, which had finished with 26 more points than us. We took them to a seventh game, which unfortunately we lost. I didn't play in Game 7. I had torn the cartilage off my rib cage. The doctors couldn't help; they couldn't even freeze it. I took the warm-up. I could have played, but I was nowhere close to my usual level. I figured as a team we would be better off, hopefully, with a healthy body in the lineup. We lost 2–1. It was really close. Did I make the right call? Who knows.

There were a lot of mixed emotions when that season ended. The playoffs proved we were becoming a better team, or so it seemed. Wendel had lived up to his potential and scored 34 goals as a rookie, and we were all focused on getting better.

But I wasn't the captain anymore. It bothers me to this day—what I did and how it was handled. Back then, though, I could only look ahead to next year. And for once, that seemed like a positive thing to do.

10

BACK WITH BROPH

When we opened the 1986–87 season, I expected Wendel Clark would be named the new captain of the Leafs.

In my opinion, he was ready for it—or as ready as you can be in Toronto. I don't know if Wendel would have accepted it, but I don't think he would have had any problems. About to turn twenty, he was already a leader. Outside distractions never seemed to bother him whatsoever. Even so, Harold was still there causing havoc, so maybe Wendel would have turned it down. Of course, he would have needed to be asked if he wanted the "C" in order to turn it down, not be told he was captain, like I was. No matter. Wendel would be captain one day, but going into the fall of 1986, we didn't have anyone wearing the "C." But we did have another new coach.

After our nice run in the spring, when there was once again an element of hope around the team, we let Dan Maloney go. We had made progress in his two seasons, so Danny wanted a two-year contract and a raise. Harold, forever cheap, wouldn't give it to him. The team offered Dan a one-year deal, and Danny ended up signing with the Winnipeg Jets. Our younger guys were probably happy to see him go, because they found his hard-ass coaching style tougher to take than the vets did. Maybe that factored in to Harold and Gerry's decision.

It didn't matter much to me who the coach was going to be. I was just happy that we were coming together as a team, and I thought that good things were going to happen in the next two or three years. As far as my run-ins with Dan were concerned, you can't hold grudges. Sure, he was giving us shit, but he'd often come to me and talk about the problems in our game that he'd been sounding off about. He was frustrated, and he needed to vent and talk.

Regardless of what I thought of Dan and his methods, I was happy for him that he got the job in Winnipeg. But for the Leafs? Here we go again. Just as we were starting to get things together as a team, just as our coach was growing and getting us to the next level and the playoffs had us all optimistic about the coming season—he's gone. We have to start over with a new coach.

The good news for me was that John Brophy was coming back to Toronto to take over. I knew Broph as a head coach from my season with the Birmingham Bulls, and I liked him a lot. He could be emotional and volatile, but he cared for his players and pushed you to be your best. He was old-school, and we could have used a more modern coach at the time, but at least we knew him. Broph had been an assistant coach with the Leafs for a couple of seasons, but he didn't like that role. And he wasn't Maloney's choice for the job. Broph preferred to run his own show. He couldn't take orders. He thought he'd be better off, and that it would be better for the organization, if he coached the farm team in St. Catharines. He took over from Claire Alexander (nicknamed the Milkman, because he once delivered milk in Orillia). When they offered Claire the assistant's job in Toronto, he turned it down. He wasn't happy they had given Broph his job. At first he left the organization but did come up to the Leafs for the rest of the season.

I was genuinely happy for Broph because I liked him, but also because he had been a minor-league lifer as a player and coach. He had a lot to do with the success of my career. And now he was getting an opportunity, for the first time ever, to coach in the NHL. He probably would have been more successful had he come in ten years earlier. He was a motivator, but by the time he arrived, the coaching world was starting to change, to rely on systems and the use of video. That's not the type of coach you got when you hired Broph. But he really cared about the guys and he wanted everyone to succeed.

Some guys didn't always understand what he wanted from them. One of those guys was Russ Courtnall. I think Russ thought Broph wanted him to be a goon, which wasn't going to happen. But that wasn't it. Broph just wanted him to give 100 percent to the game that he played. I don't think Russ could wrap his head around that, and ultimately, in part, a few seasons later it led to one of the worst trades the Leafs have ever made, dealing Russ to Montreal for tough guy John Kordic.

I understood what Broph wanted. If you were a third-line player, he didn't expect you to be a 50-goal scorer, but he did expect you to be the best damn third-line player you could be. He screamed a fair bit, but I don't know if there was a coach in the league back then who didn't yell a lot. There was no babying anybody, no kid gloves—it was go out, do your goddamn job and maximize your talent.

He did have a reputation, no question. He had some legendary rants. I remember telling some of the guys stories about Broph when he was hired. There was one when he was coaching the Voyageurs in Nova Scotia, the Canadiens' farm team. He was so pissed at a certain player that he had the driver stop the bus on the side of the highway so he could kick the kid off the bus, with his gear.

There was another story, again from when he was coaching the Voyageurs. They were in the playoffs, it was the third round, and a lot of their guys were banged up. There was a guy in a wheelchair who hung around the team all the time. Well, they lost a game at home and the guy wheels himself into the dressing room. The players were coming into the room and they told him he'd better get out of there, that Broph wasn't going to be happy. The kid tried to get out, but he couldn't do it quick enough. Broph barged in and was ranting and raving and yelling. He saw this guy in the wheelchair, grabbed the chair and pushed him out of the room. Broph said, "Get out of here. I've got enough cripples in here and don't need any more." That sounds awful, but he usually treated the kid like gold, and he was the reason the kid hung around the team. Broph just got frustrated and had a rough way of speaking that you'd expect for the times (and getting that guy out of the room before he unloaded on the team was probably a favour).

Otherwise, Broph was like every coach with the twenty-one factor: seven players love him, seven players hate him, and his job as coach

My dad, Claude, built that backyard rink in Ottawa for us every winter.

Amherst Pee Wee Macs 1969-70

My team from Nova Scotia at the famous Quebec international pee-wee tournament. I'm second from the left, back row.

Outside our house in Ottawa with my father, before his accident led us to Nova Scotia and then PEI.

Montreal hosted the 1978 World Junior Championship. Canada wore blue.

At 17, I left PEI to play junior with the Sherbrooke Castors.

Birmingham, Alabama, loved its Bulls, of the short-lived WHA.

I was drafted fifth overall in 1979 by Vancouver, but didn't stay long. The Canucks' fourth overall pick in 1978, Bill Derlago, and I were traded to Toronto in February of my rookie season.

Harold Ballard's dog, TC Puck, joins the Maple Leafs team photo.

At the young age of 22, I was named Leafs captain and scored 54 goals. My fiftieth came on a perfect pass from Bill Derlago, and got past St. Louis Blues defenceman Guy Lapointe and goalie Mike Liut.

© Frank Lennon/Getty

The late, great comic actor John Candy (left) became a close friend in Toronto. He livened up our team Halloween parties with his presence—and by letting Joyce and me into the SCTV makeup room!

Singer Anne Murray was another friend. She performed at the NHL All-Star weekend one of the years when I made the Campbell Conference team.

© All-Star James Lipa

Lucky man. With Joyce in Toronto, the night I broke Frank Mahovlich's single-season goals record.

Bill Watters (left) was my longtime agent. That's radio personality Bob McCown with us.

Signing autographs at the Rick Vaive Golf Classic in PEI. An uncle I was close to was severely disabled by cerebral palsy, and I hosted this tournament to raise money for the cause.

At the 1985 draft, I was on hand to welcome Toronto's number-one pick, Wendel Clark. King Clancy is to my right and Leafs owner Harold Ballard is beside Wendel.

In our finest with my Leafs (and former Bulls) coach John Brophy. There was nobody like "Broph."

Joyce and I out on the town with Börje and Margitta Salming, and Greg and Cindy Terrion.

Greg Terrion and I played the game hard, and it showed!

A light moment at Leafs practice with Wendel and Russ Courtnall.

© Jim Russell/Toronto Star

It was a late-night "bull session" with my former Toronto linemate John Anderson that ultimately cost me the Leafs captaincy.

Laying the lumber on my old pal Greg after I was traded to Chicago.

Neck problems caught up to me in Buffalo, my final stop in the NHL.

Joining the fun with Buffalo Bills' quarterback Jim Kelly (front, centre) after his golf tournament.

I found my love for playing hockey again in Rochester.

Amerks fit to be tied

Win 4-2 to even series with Rangers

By Kevin Oklobzija

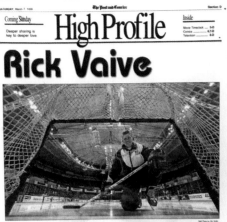

Coming Sunday
Deeper sharing is
key to deeper love

High Profile

Inside
Movie Timeclock 8-D
Comics 6,7-D
Television 8-D

Rick Vaive

Rick Vaive faces into the net at the North Charleston Coliseum.

Stingrays' coach finds what's important in life

The ECHL expansion South Carolina Stingrays made me their first head coach. We loved everything about living in Charleston, especially the championship we won in 1997.

My last big coaching job was with Don Cherry (to my right), who owned the OHL Mississauga Ice Dogs. The job didn't last. The great Bobby Orr (centre) and a very good coach I never saw eye-to-eye with in Chicago, Mike Keenan (rear).

Sharing a moment with some fellow former Leafs captains (add a defenceman and we'd make one heck of a power play): Wendel Clark, Doug Gilmour and Darryl Sittler.

How things change. Joyce, our sons, Justin and Jeff, and me… the small guy!

Born in 2019, Jeff's son and our first grandchild, Hunter. He looks good in blue and white.

is to keep the other seven players away from the guys who hate him. I think a lot of people—some players, fans, people in the organization—looked at him and thought, *Oh gawd, John Brophy's the coach.* I just tried to keep the team from getting down about the change. I told the guys: You can't judge someone on old stories, stuff you don't know. Give him a chance. You've never played for him but he won in the minors and we're coming off a pretty good finish. So we all just have to work.

We had some good momentum, and we actually got off to a good start that year. We were 7-2-3 in early November. The last game before Christmas I scored in overtime in Minnesota and we were in first place in our division. Of course, it was the Norris Division, and we were .500 to start the new calendar year.

There was a sad side to that good start. King Clancy, who had been a star player in the league back in the day and then a referee before spending years with the Leafs in many different jobs—mostly as Harold's sidekick in the later years—got sick and died in early November. He was a wonderful person, loved by all.

He was the one who kept Harold in check, especially after Harold's wife passed away. They used to watch the games together in Harold's bunker at the northeast end of the Gardens. King hung out with him all the time, especially on the road, and helped Harold keep his diabetes in check. King was a great person. He came to the rink every day with a smile on his face. He just loved to be around the guys. We talked a lot. He and Harold would have their friendly arguments—it went on all the time; they would bicker about one thing or the other—but at the end they'd walk out together and everything was good.

After King was gone... that's when Harold got a little crazy. Or crazier. He closed the bunker as a tribute. It was tough on Harold. The two of them had been joined at the hip for so many years, and then all of a sudden both his wife and best friend were gone. Without the two people in his life who seemed to stabilize him, Harold didn't cope very well.

On the ice, that season saw the emergence of the Hound Line—which was Wendel, Gary Leeman and Courtnall, who had all played for the Notre Dame College Hounds in the Saskatchewan junior league. That line had some success. Both Wendel and Gary were defencemen who were moved to the wings. It was Broph's idea to put Gary on right wing, and it was a great move. They were all good players and had a chemistry together. They fed off each other. It was another reason to believe that we could get better, and although Russ was having a hard time with Broph, he still got his points. He didn't seem to get along with any of the coaches. I don't know why. I guess you had to treat him with kid gloves, and that's how you'd get the best out of him, but he wasn't going to get any of that from our bench.

Tom Fergus was my centre at the time, and we had a lot of different guys on the left side, but I still managed 32 goals. I was still hurting, with my nagging hip problems and charley horses. I had the neck pain that I couldn't figure out, too, and that rash, which came and went. I'd been knocked out a few times in my career, but maybe the scariest was at the Gardens one night (I don't remember exactly when, go figure) when I got pulled off my feet while driving hard to the net. I went headfirst into the post, and that was when the nets didn't come off easily. I went to the hospital—Joyce was with me—and the doctor asked what had happened. I told him I was trying to get the birds in the nest. I meant to say I was trying to get the puck in the net. I'd been pretty durable as a pro, missing only a handful of games each year. But I played just 61 games that season, fewer than any of my NHL seasons to that point.

As we expected, partway through the year Broph decided he wanted the team to be tougher, so he called up Val James from the farm team. Val had been drafted by Detroit in the sixteenth round in 1977, played seven games with Buffalo in 1981–82 (zero points, 16 penalty minutes) and came over to the Leafs organization. He played hard, was tough and was a fighter. So Broph called him up, and the first day in practice he got Val to stand in front of the net. Broph was angry because our defence had something like two hits all night in the previous game. Broph calls "my no-hit defencemen" to gather around the front of the net. He says, "A fifty-three-year-old man is going to show you how to play defence and clear the front of the fucking net." He cross-checked Val and whacked him across the legs and worked him over until Val finally went down. It took some work, though; he was tough. And Broph says, "That's how you do it." Given what's happened in the hockey world in recent times with abusive coaches, that certainly wouldn't happen today, or at least it wouldn't be tolerated. But I know that Broph loved Val. He'd had him in St. Catharines, where he'd managed three assists in a full season, and he wanted him to stick in Toronto. But he just wasn't skilled enough to play in the NHL.

Val played four games, had 16 penalty minutes, very few shifts. I felt bad for him. It wasn't fair of Broph to do something like that, but that was Broph. And Val had to take it because, back then, the easiest way to get a ticket back to the minors was to argue with the coach. On that team, there were probably four guys on one-way contracts, meaning you got paid your NHL salary even if you were sent to the minors. So everyone else could easily be sent down to Newmarket (during the off-season, our AHL farm team had moved there from St. Catharines). And no one wanted to go down—not just because you'd be riding the buses, but because your salary could go from, say, $90,000 to $20,000, and that's a big hit.

There are a couple other Broph moments worth telling, even though I wasn't on the team when they happened. One was after a game on February 22, 1988, in Minnesota (that place was not Leaf-friendly!). The Leafs stunk the joint out, lost 4–2, and after the game Broph didn't say much to the media—it was a mini tirade. He was steaming. The press conference lasted just a minute or so and the reporters left to go into the dressing room. Next thing you know, Broph had his assistant coach go into the room to get the reporters. He was ready to talk. Well, he started on a major tirade (he apparently said one particular expletive seventy-two times in a four-minute span). It was a rant—justified—about taking pride in yourself, in the sweater you wear, your teammates, everything. And he talked about how privileged all of us were to be in the NHL, players and coaches. He never took being in the NHL for granted. He took so much pride in doing his job, and he expected everyone to do the same. Of course, every team had two or three guys who did take it for granted, who didn't give a shit, and that just drove him crazy.

Another famous incident happened on December 1, 1988. And it says a lot about Broph. This one happened in Los Angeles, at the old Fabulous Forum. To get to the ice, the players had to walk down a long hall from the dressing room and come out in the corner of the rink. The coaches could do the same, but that meant walking along the ice to get to the bench. Some coaches would walk under the collapsible metal stands to get to the bench. But you had to really duck under the bleachers, otherwise you could bang your head. Well, Broph decided to take the shortcut, came up a little early and banged his head.

Here he is: Broph, with his white hair, wearing a stylish light-silver jacket, bleeding like crazy. Blood everywhere. But he refused to leave to get stitched up. The TV cameras kept showing him pressing a towel to his head, blood running down the side of his face and all over his shirt and jacket. Mark Osborne had the great quote: "With that white hair and all that blood, he looked like the Japanese flag." But that was Broph. That's how he played; that's the type of guy he was.

Speaking of blood, that 1986–87 season had one of the scariest moments I've witnessed in hockey. It was late November. We were playing in Detroit, there was a scramble in front of our net, and somehow Gerard Gallant's skate cut Börje's face. It was a massive cut. It was ugly. I was on the bench at the time, but I could easily tell it was bad.

I've mentioned Guy Kinnear, the boat mechanic Harold hired to be our medical trainer. Well, Gunner ran down to the bench door to help Börje to the medical room, or the ambulance when it arrived. Somebody had told me previously that Gunner fainted when he saw lots of blood—and, sure enough, down he went. Bob McGill was the first guy to grab Börje; then Danny Lemelin, our equipment guy, helped him to the medical room. Meanwhile, we had to grab Gunner and get him out of the way so guys could get in and out of the bench. Somebody on the end of the bench pulled smelling salts out of the pouch Gunner had on his belt, waved it under his nose and said, "Come on, Gunner, get up. We might need you."

Börje was fortunate. The cut snaked up from the right side of his mouth and along the side of his nose, but somehow—and I'd say miraculously—around the inside of the eye socket, up onto his forehead. The first thing that went through the mind, obviously, was to hope Börje was going to be okay. It was pretty scary, and we were all thinking about that eye, his face covered in blood. When we saw him the next day, all stitched up, well, thank God on both fronts. It's probably a good thing it happened in Detroit—Murder City—because that plastic surgeon had probably sewn up more than a few knife wounds in his day. He did a helluva job. That scar is barely visible. The doctors estimated he needed 250 stitches, because there was so much stitching done inside and outside.

Steve Thomas had the best description of Börje's face after we met up with him the next day. He said that with all the stitching it looked like a softball. I remember thinking I should put on a visor. I had that same reaction every time someone got cut in the face. I thought to myself, *I should put one on.* And I did—on and off again.

As for the rest of the season, in January we ran into a bunch of injuries and hit the skids, winning just two of 11 games. The worst loss during that stretch was a game at home against Calgary. We led

5–0 after the first period. We led 5–0 after the second. We led 5–0 until the 6:02 mark of the third period. We lost 6–5 in overtime. It was one of those nights when everything starts to fall apart and you just can't stop it. They got the first one, scored another a few minutes later, and we all started running around. Then they get the next one and it's crazy in your own end and you can't stop them.

We ended up winning three of our last five games of the season, and four of six, to get into the playoffs. We finished tied with Minnesota with 70 points, but won the tiebreaker because we had two more wins. That meant we faced St. Louis, which had finished first in the Norris Division. A little perspective: the Blues had the same number of wins as us, 32, and no team in the Chuck Norris Division, as it was called back then for the tough play, had a winning record. Sure, we played in a weak division, but year over year we had climbed from 48 points to 57 to 70. That was a good thing. We were headed in the right direction, however slowly.

And that spring we played well. We lost the first game in St. Louis but managed a 3–2 win to go home tied. We lost Game 3 at home, so we trailed 2–1, but then won the next three in a row: 2–1, 2–1, 4–0. For a team that had finished eighteenth out of twenty-one teams in goals against, tightening up like that was impressive. Ken Wregget, one of our young goalies, played really well.

Anytime you played St. Louis, it wasn't easy. Every team was physical back then, but I had to play against Brian Sutter, who was one of the toughest guys I'd ever seen. We never fought—although I'm sure there were times when we could have—but the hacking and whacking, the hooking and grabbing, and the physical play was going to be even worse in the playoffs than the refs would allow during the season. I'd give it back to him, there was a mutual respect, but due to injury Brian was out of the playoffs. Still St. Louis were tough, and they had Rob Ramage. After the game, he and I might go grab a bite to eat, but during the game it was a battle. I think he broke a few sticks over my arms. I don't think I ever broke one over him, but it wasn't for lack of trying—my sticks were just too thick and stiff.

Broph debuted a new look for Game 1 of that series. He showed up on the bench wearing a black fedora. Everyone's looking at him, thinking, *What the hell is that?* But one thing about John, he was always trying to do something different, to mix things up, so you didn't get into a rut. The black hat was meant to lighten things up, get us to relax.

In Game 6, we won 4–0 at the Gardens to take the series. All night long the crowd was chanting for Brad Smith—Motor City Smitty. He was a hard-working utility guy, a heart-and-soul player who endeared himself to the fans. Well, Smitty opened the scoring that night and the place went nuts. All night the fans were chanting his name. But Broph had decided he wasn't going to play. We had built up our lead and he wasn't taking any chances; he was shortening the bench. In the third period, there was a TV timeout, and Broph sent Smitty over the boards to take a twirl. He charged down the ice and gave Kenny Wregget a big pat on the pads, then raced back to the bench. Broph wanted him to have his curtain call, and he wanted to fire up the building and the bench. As I've said, Broph understood motivation.

We continued our roll into the next round against the Red Wings, winning the first two games in Detroit. We lost Game 3 again at home, but beat them 3–2 in overtime—Mike Allison with the winner—to take a 3–1 series lead back to Joe Louis Arena. At that point, we had won six of our last seven games. We were in total control of the series, but it just turned on us. They won the next game 3–0; we came home for Game 6 and lost 4–2. Now we had to go back there for Game 7.

There were a few sideshows during that series. Gerry McNamara's contract was up, and I'm sure he was expecting a raise and an extension. Behind his back, we sometimes called Gerry B.D., because a story had come out in the newspapers that he was suing after being in a car accident, claiming he had suffered brain damage. Our general manager was publicly claiming he had *brain damage!* Most of the time, also behind his back, we just called him Fish, after a character on the sitcom *Barney Miller*, played by actor Abe Vigoda. They walked the same way, looked the same. Harold responded to Gerry's desire for a new contract in his usual manner. He went to the papers and questioned Gerry's ability.

As we were leaving Toronto for one of the games in Detroit, Börje was late for the charter. Broph said, "We're leaving." We're thinking, *He's our best defenceman, it would be nice to have him along for the trip.* "Nope, we're leaving." And we could see Börje out on the tarmac. We almost left without him.

For Game 7, we dressed Miro Ihnačák—Peter's brother—wearing 27, of all numbers. Back in 1985, the Leafs had gotten Miro out of Czechoslovakia, which was still a communist country, and they spent a lot of money doing it. While Peter was a good player, Miro wasn't. He played 34 games in the 1986–87 season, but just one in the playoffs: Game 7 in Detroit. Nothing against him, but around the team, and in the media, it felt like he was being inserted into the lineup and was supposed to make a difference. He didn't.

Earlier in the series, I'd gotten into a scuffle and hit the glass with a punch. It broke my hand. Our doctors froze the hand, and I went back out and finished the game. For some reason, though, our regular doctors didn't come with us on the trip for Game 7. We had a Detroit doctor, who put in one little shot of freezing, just one spot instead of freezing the whole hand. Halfway through the first period, the freezing started to wear off and I couldn't even grab my stick. Basically, I warmed the bench for the rest of the game. I had a few shifts, but I couldn't do anything. That was frustrating. We ended up getting shut out in two of the last three games of the series, including Game 7, 3–0.

In any series, Game 7 is pretty much a flip of the coin. The teams have both figured out how to beat each other if they've pushed the series that far. Unfortunately, the coin flipped on Detroit's side. If we'd found a way to win one more game, we would have been in the conference final—only the second time the Leafs had gone that far since the '67 Cup. It would have been fantastic. Disappointed as we were, we were all pretty excited about the season ahead.

But of course, I wouldn't be there to join them.

11

THE NEW GUY (CHICAGO)

Looking back at my time with the Maple Leafs, many of those teams weren't very close off the ice, at least at first. Because we weren't often good, it felt like a lot of the guys were playing for themselves, and that's a recipe for disaster. And in large part, we weren't close as a group because we used to charter most of the time. We'd mostly fly in the night before a game, then fly out after the game. One year, Harold got pissed with a flight attendant—she was handing out chocolate bars but wouldn't give him one because he was diabetic—so he cancelled the Air Ontario charters. It was a pain in the ass to fly commercial, having to go through those air-port lineups day after day, but it also meant the guys got to know each other better. We would have dinners and hang out a lot more after games. Back then, we didn't know a lot about sports science and what drinking did to your body and performance levels; that most times after a night out on the town, it affected you more the second day than it did the first. Sometimes, two days later your legs would feel like cement blocks.

Billy Derlago, Danny Daoust, Greg Terrion, Terry Martin, John Anderson, Börje Salming and me, we hung out a lot. Our group was close. I used to drive with Greg to the rink every day. Börje and Dave Hutchinson were close in age and had played together for two seasons in the late seventies with the Leafs, so when Hutchy came back in 1983–84, they hung out and led the charge to the bars. They'd get the guys together after practices or games, which wasn't a bad thing, but it led to a lot more drinking and late nights than it should have.

I wasn't out with them all the time, but I was with them often enough. I would try to leave early—same with the lunches. When you're the captain, you kind of have to be there, or at least I felt that way. Whether it was a lunch or after a game, you'd socialize, have a few. On days off, when I didn't go to the rink, I didn't drink much at home. Joyce was a social drinker, at most. If we went out, she'd have a couple of glasses of wine, and that would pretty much be it.

I couldn't put it away like some of the guys, and it would affect me more than it did many of them. I could get sloppy. Going out with my teammates got me into a jam most of the time, because it got me drinking more than I could manage. But I felt I had to be there because I was the captain. Another Catch 22.

That pressure to be there let up after I lost the captaincy, but by then I was pretty set in my ways. But I wasn't long for the team.

As disappointing as that loss to Detroit was in the 1987 playoffs—especially after leading 3–1 in the series and being just a win away from the conference final—I still ended that year pretty excited. It felt like we were making strides as a team and had some good young talent to build around. I was thinking, *If we can make the right changes, this team could take the next step.*

And then September 3 came around. I had no inkling of what was coming.

It was just a few days before training camp opened in Toronto. I was playing in a Leaf sponsors golf tournament at Horseshoe Valley, which is about an hour and a half's drive north of the city, at least when the traffic co-operates. The 1987 Canada Cup was on at the time, but I hadn't been invited despite having some pretty good seasons. I had been invited to the Team Canada camp in 1984, but I didn't make the team. Glen Sather was the coach, and John Muckler was the assistant. Sather and I had that history dating back to our WHA days.

During that '84 camp, we were in Banff and Edmonton, and we had an exhibition game one night. I had a bad sinus infection, but I was still supposed to play. I told them I would if they really wanted me to, but I'd rather not play because I didn't want to go out and look shitty and hurt my chances of making the team. I don't think Sather and Muckler were too happy about that. I got cut and I was upset about it, but I also knew that even though I may have been better than some players they kept, those guys were all great. That team was dominated by the Oilers and Islanders, who were winning the Stanley Cup at the time. I really wasn't surprised when I wasn't invited in 1987. Again, there was so much great talent and my goal numbers had fallen off a bit, but also the tournament was run by Alan Eagleson, who had been my agent until Bill Watters split to start his own agency and I'd left to go with Bill. That couldn't have helped my chances.

Anyway, it was after I had finished playing at the golf tournament that Bill Watters told me that Bob McGill, Steve Thomas and I had been traded to Chicago for Ed Olczyk and Al Secord.

That was probably the most pissed off I've been in my life. I had no idea. Later, I was told that a certain reporter who is contributing to this book had written in the morning newspaper that the trade was coming that day. Of course, back then, we didn't have social media or cellphones, and the internet didn't exist, at least for the public. So I had no inkling whatsoever that the trade was in the works. I hadn't heard any talk about it.

What a disappointment. I didn't want to leave Toronto. I loved it there. The team was starting to evolve and get better. I'd lost the captaincy, but it didn't matter. I was still committed to the team. But maybe the general manager, Gerry McNamara, felt differently. I think he had a big hand in the decision to take away the "C."

I still don't really know why that trade was made. Part of it may have been John Brophy, who always wanted more toughness, although I played a pretty hard-nosed game. I don't know how much say Broph had in the deal, but I know he loved Secord. Al had been a helluva player, a 54-goal scorer one season playing alongside Denis Savard, my future centre, and Steve Larmer. But Al was kind of finished with fighting at that point in his career, certainly the year after the trade. He was older. He didn't want to fight anymore.

Eddie was a really good player, and he came in and played well for Toronto. The Leafs had always liked Eddie O. A year earlier, Leafs defenceman Gary Nylund, a third overall pick in 1982, who like so many in Toronto was rushed into the lineup before he was ready, signed an offer sheet with Chicago as a restricted free agent. Harold Ballard, naturally, refused to match the offer. I believe it was for $620,000 over three years. As compensation, the Hawks offered the Leafs centre Ken Yaremchuk, defenceman Jerome Dupont and a fourth-round draft pick. The Leafs asked for Eddie, who was just twenty years old and had scored 79 points the season before. Instead, arbitrator Ed Houston opted for the Hawks' offer and awarded the two players and the pick. There was a report in a Chicago newspaper that Harold told Broph that neither Ken nor Jerome was good enough to play in Toronto and he should send them to the minors. Typical.

I can only imagine what would have happened if the Leafs had gotten Eddie then. I might have been in Toronto for another three or four years and seen some better results for the team, because Eddie would have been a really good addition. I don't know why the trade happened as it did. You've got someone—me—who had scored 30-plus goals for seven straight seasons, including the three 50-plus-goal seasons, and you trade him. Stumpy (Thomas) had scored 35 goals the previous year, but he was involved in a contract dispute. And Bobby was a tough kid the Leafs had invested some time in developing.

I was bitter. I was really angry and disappointed. To this day I'm disappointed about it, especially with how the next six years unfolded. The first year in Chicago was decent, but after that, everything went downhill.

After Bill broke the news, I left the tournament before the dinner and headed home. I had to pack up the car over the next day and drive to Chicago. The worst part was leaving my wife and two-year-old kid, knowing they wouldn't be with me in Chicago until sometime in October. Joyce had to stay behind, look after Jeff, sell the house, get the movers in and get all our possessions packed up. She had to do everything on her own. It was a lot, but we both had to somehow find a way to get through that period. We didn't see each other for more than a month. It worked out, but it's not something you want to put your family through, let's put it that way.

I'd been traded twice now, and this time felt different. When you're traded, you don't really feel like a piece of meat, like you might think, but in my playing days a trade did put a few things in perspective. You are an asset, and for most players the team can do whatever they want with you, whenever they want to do it. You have no control over where you're going to live and work. You just go where you're told, and you play. The situation is different for some players today, with no-trade and no-move clauses and lists of teams they won't play for, but back then, any sort of control over your future was rare.

At the time of my first trade, from Vancouver to Toronto, I was young and headed to a big hockey city, so that was kind of neat. I was a little scared at first, of course, because it happened during my rookie season, but I quickly embraced the move. I didn't have a family yet, so I just packed up what I had and got on the plane. And I also wasn't leaving a city I'd grown attached to. Finding the positive in this new trade was a little harder, but there was a silver lining. It was hard saying goodbye to teammates and friends and leaving a city Joyce and I loved, but there was a nice financial gain. I was in the last year of my Leafs contract and making $300,000. I think we received thirteen cheques in a season, so in Toronto, after taxes, I was taking home about $11,000 per cheque. Today, all NHL players are paid in US dollars, but back then players on Canadian teams were paid in Canadian dollars, and taxes were much lower in the States. With the move to Chicago, I effectively got a raise. When I got my first paycheque, I thought the Hawks had made a mistake. I took it to the business office and they said, "No, that's the right number." It was more than $16,000—which meant I was earning something like $5,000 or $6,000 more every two weeks. As I mentioned, cars were my weak spot and I'd always wanted to own a Mercedes 420 SCL, but I couldn't afford one in Toronto. In Chicago, that changed. I was twenty-eight years old and walked into a dealership wearing a pair of jeans and a T-shirt. There were all these old salesmen sitting around and not a single one got up to help me. I decided to go to another dealership and the salesmen there greeted me the same way. They didn't move. They must have been thinking that this kid in jeans and a T-shirt couldn't afford a Mercedes.

A week or so later, I went back to the first dealership. This young guy—he was maybe my age or a little older—came over and asked if he could help. I said, "Yeah, I want to buy that car right there." He asked if I wanted to lease it. I said, "No, I want to buy it." He says, "Well, it costs $62,000." I said, "It costs that right now, but by the time we finish talking it won't." I got him down to $58,500. I wrote a cheque, got my car, and as I drove past the front of the dealership all the old guys were standing at the window gawking at me. I gave them a wave, probably a finger too.

During training camp, we all stayed downtown at the Bismarck Hotel, which was owned by Bill Wirtz, the owner of the Hawks.

There were always a lot of guys around, so that made the adjustment to a new team easier. We went to a Bears football game together, did a bunch of things as a group. But the move was still tough. You're in a strange city, you've got to find out where everything is, how to get to the rink, to the airport, all those things. The hockey made it easier—when I was at the rink or on the road, I could just concentrate on my job. In my spare time, though, I had to find my family a house. I was looking out in Wheaton, a suburb about an hour's drive from the old Chicago Stadium, where Denis Savard lived.

It took a little while, but I finally found a beautiful house and bought it. We loved the neighbourhood, and Denis lived just around the corner. He's such a nice guy, and he wanted to help me settle in. He was like that with everyone. He's one of those guys—and you hear this said all the time, but it was true about him—who would give you the shirt off his back. His wife, Mona, was the same. She was so generous with her time and helped Joyce find everything in the area and the city. Denis and I drove together to the rink every day. The two of them made the transition so much easier. I lived in the hotel for a while, and then moved in with them until our house was ready. It was really nice when Joyce and Jeff arrived. We could finally settle in and feel at home.

It took longer to feel at home with the team. You know—you're the new guy, and no one really wants to let you into their world right away. I needed time to get to know the guys and build that trust. I remember we were on a western road trip, out in Calgary and Edmonton, and we had a few days between games, so we went to Banff. One day, after practice, we came across a curling rink next door to the arena we were using. Eight of us walked in to have a look, and the next thing you know we're all on the ice, in our nice dress shoes, trying to curl. A guy showed up at the door, saw us and then closed the door. We thought, *Oh shit, we're going to get kicked out.* But a few minutes later the door opens again and in he comes with a great big tray of beer. He says, "Have fun, boys!" So here we are, eight of us idiots in our fancy dress shoes, drinking beer and curling and having a great time for two and half hours. Stuff like that helps bring guys together, and I found the Blackhawks to be a really great bunch. Thank goodness nobody got hurt.

I spent a lot of time with Savvy off the ice, but I also got to play with him right from the start. He was an amazing talent. He had great speed and great skill. He was a terrific passer, and he could finish, too. He was one of those players who you'd sometimes find yourself watching when you were on the ice, because he did so many special things. Fans of a certain vintage will remember the amazing move he used to make. He'd fly up the ice, weaving through traffic, cross the blue line, and as he was approaching the defence he'd jump and do a spin-around move. The Savardian Spin-o-rama—although that name was originally given, by broadcasting great Danny Gallivan, to a move perfected by legendary Canadiens defenceman Serge Savard.

Savvy was hard to play with at first because he loved to dangle the puck and make so many moves. I was used to playing with Dan Daoust, Billy Derlago and Tom Fergus—for the most part, I'd come late and get the puck on the fly. It was the same when I played with Wayne Gretzky at the 1982 World Championships. It took me a while to get used to playing with Savvy because he always made that extra move. When Denis had the puck he was electric. I remember one game, playing Edmonton at home. He got the puck above the faceoff circle, beat five guys—to make matters worse, he beat one guy twice—all in one zone, walked in and scored. I couldn't help but watch and admire it.

I was glad for him when he got traded to Montreal later in his career and won the Stanley Cup, in 1993. I wish it had happened earlier for him, because he didn't play in that Cup-winning game. He was in and out of the lineup all season. It would have been better if it had happened a year or two earlier and he'd been able to play a bigger part. But it was great to see him on the ice with the Cup, especially winning it with his hometown team. The guys you play with—you hope almost everybody gets a chance to do that. Savvy ended up playing another five seasons, which was a little bit surprising because we figured he was near the end, but it was really nice that he played his final three years back in Chicago and was able to retire as a Blackhawk.

The third member of our line was Steve Larmer, our left winger. Larms was a great player and a great guy. It was almost a contest between the two of us to see who got to the rink the earliest on game days. On the road, we'd leave the hotel before the team bus, but we never left together. Finally I said, "Larms, why don't we just go together? Why don't we take a cab together? We're wasting money!" If it was a seven o'clock game, I was usually at the rink around 4 p.m., and he was usually there five minutes before me. "Let's share a cab, save a few bucks, and I'll even let you walk in the door first."

His nickname was Grandpa: he was quiet, content to just sit and watch TV or what have you, like a grandpa. But could he play!

He was a terrific two-way player, could skate, could play in all three zones. Every year when they announce the inductees into the Hockey Hall of Fame, people wonder why Larms has never made it. I think his numbers certainly put him in the conversation, especially when you factor in how complete his game was. He had 441 goals and 1,012 points in 1,006 games. His 884-game iron-man streak in the regular season is the third-longest in NHL history, behind Doug Jarvis's 964 and Garry Unger's 914. He won the Calder Trophy, and then the Stanley Cup with the Rangers in 1994. If you talk to anyone who played on that team they will tell you picking up Larms that season was huge. When he retired in 1995, he had one year left on a pretty good contract in New York, but he just packed it in.

The chances of him getting into the Hall of Fame are probably slim because it's been so many years since he played, but you never know. With his numbers, there's no argument in my mind. He should be in there with Savvy.

That first season in Chicago, our line did well. Looking back, it's funny, all three of us were smokers. The coaches called us the Marlboro Line after the brand of cigarettes. We smoked before games, we'd light up in the bathroom between periods. Despite that, we finished one-two-three in team scoring. Savvy had 44 goals and 131 points, Larms had 41 goals and 89 points, and I had 43 goals and 69 points in 76 games. That was 128 goals between us. All in all it was a good year, but it's never a really good year unless you win.

As fate would have it, our first game of the season was against the Leafs, which was a little weird. We ended up losing 7–5.

The first time I went back to Toronto? It sucked, actually, because I still wanted to be playing there, and now I'm on the visiting team and the fans are booing me. I had hoped it wouldn't be like that. There were some cheers, but it was nothing like it is today with the video tributes. Of course, there weren't any video scoreboards back then! But the attitude was different, too. I remember that night I had a fight with Danny Daoust. It wasn't much of a fight—we went hard into the boards and just grabbed on to each other. His job was to shut down the top line. He was doing his job and I was trying to do mine. We ended up losing that one too, 6-5.

I couldn't get number 22 in Chicago because Gary Nylund had it. I asked him, and he wouldn't give it to me. So I said I wanted to wear 44, but Bob Pulford, the GM, who was old school, didn't want me to wear a high number like that. He said, "You don't want to draw any more attention to yourself after a big trade." I said, "Pully, it's just a number. It doesn't matter what number I'm wearing. I can't see it when I'm playing." But he wouldn't agree, so I wore 27.

Our coach was Bob Murdoch, whose nickname was Mud. He was a defenceman who'd played with Montreal, LA, Atlanta and then Calgary. After he retired, he served as an assistant coach with the Flames for five years before he was hired by the Hawks as the head coach. Wayne Thomas, the former goalie, and Darryl Sutter, the former Hawks great who had just retired, were the assistants. Mud lasted only the one season in Chicago, but he went on to win the Jack Adams Award as coach of the year with Winnipeg. He was a good coach, but we just didn't get the job done.

We finished with a 30-41-9 record, which was underachieving when you consider our talent. In the playoffs, we lost to St. Louis in the first round in five games. As a team, we scored 17 goals in the series and I had six of them, so not a bad showing. But anytime you lose it sucks. When you expect to win, it's even worse. The Blues had a good team, no question, but I thought ours was better.

Mud was a quiet guy, and I saw him lose it big time only once, and that was in the old St. Louis Arena during the final game of that playoff series. We were trailing 3–1 in the series and were down 3–1 after the first period. He came into the room and started throwing things around, yelling and screaming. We're all looking at each other thinking, *What the hell is going on here? This isn't the time to panic.* Then he went across the hall into the coaches' room and slammed the door behind him. We were out on the ice before the start of the second period, and I remember looking over and seeing that there weren't any coaches on the bench. *Where the hell are the coaches?* we wondered. Turns out Mud slammed the door so hard that it got jammed and they couldn't get it to open. The arena staff had to get a forklift and use the forks on the front to punch in the door. We told the officials to go ahead and drop the puck, that we could go ahead without the coaches. I scored twice in the second period and we were tied going into the third, but Brett Hull, who was a killer in that series, scored fifteen seconds in and we wound up losing 5–3. Series over. We saw the video with the forklift after the game. Despite everything on the line, it had been a funny moment when the coaches finally appeared on the bench.

We had some characters on that team. One was Behn Wilson, a big six-foot-three, 220-pound defenceman from Toronto. He was a heck of a player, but he was also arguably one of the tougher guys in the league, and he was crazy. His eyes would roll up into his head when he got mad. You didn't want any part of him when that happened. But then, after the game, you'd see him walk out of the rink and meet up with his three daughters, these cute little redheads. His wife was petite. Off the ice, he was the quietest guy in the world, and a smart guy too. But put him in his hockey equipment and he became a different person. I didn't have to play against him, at least. He was one of those guys—the type that if you got around him he'd two-hand you, or if you scored on him he'd come up to you and say, "If you do that again, the next time I'm going to cut your eye out." And he'd have meant it.

We had a really good young defenceman on our team—Bruce Cassidy. You may recognize the name: he's the very successful coach of the Boston Bruins. He was a damn good defenceman, but unfortunately he blew his knee out in junior playing with the Ottawa 67's, and his skating suffered because of it. He was a magician with the puck. He'd play the point on the power play, and everything would slow down when he got the puck. He'd handle it and make a smart play. He didn't play a lot of games, but you could see how talented he was. When he was coming out of junior, everyone was talking about him being the next Bobby Orr. He had great numbers in junior, 111 points one season, 95 the next. But his skating after the knee injury just wasn't quite what it used to be.

Another character and good player in Chicago was defenceman Marc Bergevin, who is now the general manager of the Canadiens. He was a good guy—never shut up. He'd talk and talk and talk. And he'd pull pranks. He would nail guys' shoes to the floor. He would tie your pants in a knot. But no one ever thought it was actually him doing it.

The summer leading into that 1987–88 season, the Hawks had made a big splash when they signed goaltender Bob Mason. He was coming off a terrific year in Washington. He'd been in goal for that marathon playoff game against the New York Islanders in the spring of 1987. That game—dubbed the Easter Epic—went into quadruple overtime, one of the longest games ever, but Mase and the Caps wound up losing on Pat LaFontaine's goal. He was also named to the American team for the '87 Canada Cup that fall. It was a big deal bringing him to Chicago.

Problem was, Mase didn't get off to a good start and the fans started ed booing him, so he had to play most of his games on the road. He played 41 games, but he won only 13 and had a 4.15 goals-against average. He ended up getting traded to Quebec after the season. Then there was Darren Pang, who is now a television broadcaster in St. Louis. That was his rookie season, and the Chicago fans loved him. He claimed he was five foot five, 155 pounds, but I'm not sure he was even that big. His numbers weren't great, either, but he was fearless and fun to watch, and he came up with some big games for us.

There's one night with Panger I'll never forget. We were in Hartford and were having a rookie party at a bar. Jägermeister, the liqueur, was a big thing at the time. Someone ordered a tray of shots (not the first of the night), and the rookies all had to do one. I don't remember who, but somebody was chewing tobacco and using a shot glass to spit in. The glass was just sitting on the table, and when the waitress brought the tray she unloaded the drinks around that glass of spit, not knowing what was in it. When it was Darren's turn to have a shot, he happened to grab that one and chug it back. Well, the little guy turned green and bolted to the bathroom. I think he puked for half an hour. We were laughing our asses off. Great guy, funny guy, always laughing and smiling. He could and still does light up a room. He was like the Energizer bunny from those battery commercials on television—he would go, go, go...

We had fun together and we brawled together. One Saturday night in Washington in December 1987, we were losing by a goal at the end of the third, but there was no time left on the clock. We'd lost the game. So as one of their guys, Bengt-Ake Gustafsson, was going around me, I slashed him. He went down like he was shot. Everyone on the ice started fighting. The linesman grabbed me in this big scrum. I was down on my knees. I glanced across to the other end of the pile and there was Scott Stevens. The next thing I saw was his fist coming through the pile. He got me right on the nose. It didn't really hurt, no more than a punch in the nose usually does. There were a few drops of blood on my sweater. After the game, I went to shave, looked in the mirror and saw that my nose was spread flat across my face. The doctor straightened it out. We played at home the next night and I wore a full shield. I probably broke my nose fifteen times.

Our owner was Bill Wirtz, who many in the hockey world said was Chicago's version of Harold Ballard. I don't think he was quite as crazy as Harold, but he did have some peculiarities, I suppose. First of all, his nickname in the media was Dollar Bill, because the fans and media thought he was cheap. They blamed him for a lot of good players leaving town, including the great Bobby Hull, who was lost to the WHA. Wirtz was crucified for years for "living in the Dark Ages" because he wouldn't allow the Hawks home games to be televised in Chicago, over concerns it would cannibalize ticket sales. He later put them on a pay channel.

Bill had taken over the team from his father, Arthur, who was the founder of the Wirtz Corporation, which owned the team through a holding company. Wirtz Corp. had a realty wing and a liquor business that controlled a third of the Chicago market. People believed Bill was a billionaire, which made fans even angrier to think he might be compromising the team to save money. It didn't help that the Hawks hadn't won a Stanley Cup since 1961. Wirtz also served for years as chairman of the NHL's board of governors and was a good friend of league president John Ziegler and Players' Association boss Alan Eagleson. Strange bedfellows, indeed!

We didn't see Wirtz very often. When we did, he seemed like a pretty nice man who loved his team. He could be ruthless at times, I was told, but he could also be fiercely and sometimes blindly loyal. He was certainly loyal to his GM, Bob Pulford, who as a player had starred for years with the Maple Leafs and was a good friend of Eagleson's. Anyway, Pully was a good hockey man, but I don't think he liked to spend money either. Maybe that endeared him to Wirtz. I actually think Wirtz would have done what it took to win, but it was Pully who was more like Harold when it came to spending.

At the end of the 1987–88 season, my contract was up. I was coming off a 43-goal season, and Pully offered me three years at $260,000, $260,000 and $265,000—so a $40,000 pay cut the first two seasons, $35,000 the third. Nice. The negotiations went on all summer, and finally Bill Watters got an arbitration date set. Two days before the hearing, Pully called Bill and said, "You know what's going to happen if this goes to arbitration." Bill said, "Yes, you're going to trade him." Bill called his bluff. The next day I had a new contract: $325,000, $325,000 and $350,000. Why it went on all summer long is beyond me.

I liked playing in Chicago, but I didn't really like living there. It was just such a big city. Toronto was big too, but Chicago felt bigger and busier. And it wasn't considered a big hockey town, either. Yes, it was an Original Six team and had its history, but there were the Bulls, Bears, White Sox and Cubs—four major sports teams, and we were the fifth. College sports are big there, too. I enjoyed the atmosphere in Toronto, where everything is hockey and the Maple Leafs are the hot ticket. I thrived on the pressure, never thought of it as a bad thing. I loved it. My attitude was, *Let's show them we can do it.* All those fans and the media watching us drove me to be better every day. Not everybody can play under those circumstances. You have to have thick skin to play in Toronto—same with Montreal and a lot of the other Canadian cities. There just wasn't that kind of pressure outside the rink in Chicago.

Inside was a little different. The old Chicago Stadium was a fantastic rink to play in (except for the flight of stairs between the dressing room and ice level). It was exciting, with the organ and how crazy and loud the fans got when the anthem was sung. The building was usually full, and the noise was deafening. It was fun to give that crowd something to cheer about. Unfortunately, we hadn't given them enough.

After that season, Mud was fired and Mike Keenan came in. Keenan had been fired himself in mid-May after four seasons in Philadelphia, with one year remaining on his contract. He had twice taken the Flyers—one of the youngest teams in the league—to the Stanley Cup final, where both times they lost to the Edmonton Oilers. It was an impressive run, maybe the best first four seasons of any coach in league history. But Flyers GM Bobby Clarke said he felt the team had "lost its enthusiasm" for Keenan. That's a nice way of saying the players were tired of listening to Mike and had tuned him out.

Keenan was an obvious fit in Chicago for a few reasons. One, he was an excellent and successful coach, and he had been behind the bench for Team Canada in the fall of 1987 when they won that incredible Canada Cup over the Russians. His agent was also Alan Eagleson, who was tight with Wirtz and Pully. Eagleson apparently phoned Wirtz and said, "Keenan just got fired. If you don't sign him, he's going to your rival down the road, St. Louis"—although there were also rumours he might be headed to Minnesota, maybe as GM. Anyway, Wirtz took the bait and signed him.

There were mixed feelings among the players about Mike's hiring. We knew all about his coaching tactics and the mind games he liked to play—he could be a real hard-ass—but at the same time everyone knew he was a very good coach. We were all hoping he would make us that much better. And he did some really good things that were very much needed. In some ways, he took the organization out of the Dark Ages. He set up a weight room, with bikes and all sorts of exercise equipment, which we didn't have previously. Not even the Chicago Bulls had a set-up like the one Mike put in. He also had the ashtrays removed from the dressing room! He did a lot of good stuff. He was ahead of his time in terms of conditioning and nutrition.

I didn't have a private meeting with him after he arrived, just along with the rest of the team. From the beginning, it was like I wasn't good enough to play a regular shift. Basically, he wanted me just to stand in front of the net on the power play. I was confused. I had just scored 43 goals; I was only twenty-eight years old. But Mike did things to let everybody know he was in charge. He would often battle his own best players.

I remember one time, our star defenceman Doug Wilson had a bad shoulder. It wasn't anything he couldn't play with, but it was bothering him. He wasn't having a good game one night, and Mike came in and right in front of everybody says, "Wilson, why don't you just take your gear off if you can't play?" Mike just gave it to him. That was his way of doing things: go after the big guys and let everybody know he's the boss.

It was the same thing with Denis. The day after a loss, Mike would make us skate and skate—down and back, down and back a million times. A bag skate. And Denis would always just turn when he got to the other end instead of stopping. I was on his line, so I was skating with him. Denis would turn without stopping, Mike would get pissed off, and we'd have to go again. One practice, we went fifteen times in a row because Denis wouldn't stop. Finally, one of the guys grabbed him, pushed him into the boards and made him stop. But I remember those fifteen times. My legs were cramping up—it was horrible. Savvy could skate forever.

That was an ongoing thing from the start of the season: the bag skates, the confrontations with some of the better players. I never really had a confrontation with Mike. I just did what I was told. If that's the way he wanted to play me, then okay, whatever he wants.

In mid-October, half a dozen games into the season, we had a seven-game road trip coming up. Before we left, I met with Mike. "I'm only twenty-eight years old," I said to him. "I scored 43 goals last season. I'm pretty sure I can help this team and play regular for you. Why don't you give me some games, play the shit out of me, play me on a regular shift, power play, and if I don't do whatever you think I should be doing, then do whatever you want with me. But give me an opportunity."

I was shocked when he said, "That's fair." Of course, I'm pumped because I'm going to get a chance to show him what I can do for the team. We go on the trip—Detroit, St. Louis, Pittsburgh: I didn't have a point. In Quebec, we finally won and I had a goal. Then we went to Vancouver and lost, but I had another goal. We go to Edmonton and win, 5–2, but I was minus-2. He came up to me in the airport and said, "Good game." *Wow*, I think, *I'll take whatever he gives me.* Looking back, maybe he was being sarcastic. The next night, we're in Calgary. The local TV asked me if I would be their guest during the first intermission. Back then they didn't do the interviews in the hallway. They would take you to the studio, which was just down the hall from the dressing room. Usually, they would go to the coach first and ask if they could interview a certain player. But this time they didn't, and I didn't realize that.

So I said sure, I'd do it. We start the game. I got maybe a couple of shifts and then I didn't get another one for the rest of the period. I came in after the period, threw my stuff in the room, and the runner was waiting for me in the hallway with a glass of water and a towel to take me to the studio. Mike came by and asked me where I was going. I told him I going to do the TV interview. Mike turned to the runner and said, "Let me get you someone who wants to play the game, not this fucking floater." He's standing right beside me and says that. I wanted to grab him by the throat.

To this day, I wish I had grabbed him and put him up against the wall. The fact that I didn't is one of my biggest regrets. Maybe he would have looked at me differently, because Mike liked to be challenged. He liked to see people react. I don't know if it would have helped, but I still wish I'd done it. I thought it was pretty shitty, what he did. Maybe it was just his way of saying, "I'm the boss and I don't care who you are. I'm making the decisions here." Even still . . .

I will say, though, that I don't know if I had another coach as good as Mike at running the bench. He was prepared, he was always a step ahead of the other team's coach, and I enjoyed that. It was nice to finally have a guy back there who knew what the hell he was doing. It's just too bad I spent so much time sitting in front of him.

By the way, he didn't let me do the interview.

I didn't play much on that trip, and by the time I got home I knew it was only a matter of time before I was out of there. It was just a matter of when and to where.

Fast-forward to the Christmas holidays. Joyce's parents are in town from PEI and we're playing at home on Boxing Day against St. Louis. We're on the ice for our morning skate, but Mike doesn't come out. The trainer comes up to the glass, hammers on it, and E.J. McGuire, our assistant coach—a really good guy and coach—goes down to the dressing room, comes back and approaches me.

"Mike wants to see you downstairs."

I went down to the dressing room and Mike was waiting for me.

"We just traded you to Buffalo for Adam Creighton." He added that he kind of figured I'd like to be close to Toronto for the end of my career.

"Mike, what are you talking about? I'm not from Toronto. I played there, but I'm not from there," I said. "Don't think you're doing me any favours other than getting me the fuck out of here so maybe I can play." I said what I felt. He wanted to make it sound like he was doing something nice for me, but he wasn't. I liked playing for the Hawks, though I was probably going to get a better chance to play in Buffalo.

Many years later, Mike was asked if he had a problem with me. He said he didn't, but he thought I had lost a step and he'd wanted a faster team. Not sure I agree that I couldn't keep up, and I still managed 12 goals and 25 points in 30 games of limited playing time, but Mike was the boss.

I was supposed to catch a one o'clock flight to Buffalo to play that night. So I had to drive home, get some stuff together and get to the airport. But there was a big snowstorm, so we didn't even take off until 7 p.m. It was Boxing Day, December 26, 1988. I didn't see my family again until February 5. Joyce was pregnant and Jeff was only three and a half, so that was tough on both of us. I wanted to play, but it wasn't easy being separated like that.

Looking back, absolutely everything went upside down that season in Chicago. In Wheaton, where we'd bought a house, the property taxes doubled on January 1 from $4,000 a year to $8,000. All of a sudden, there were twenty or so houses for sale in our neighbourhood. Wayne Presley asked me if I was selling the house. I told him I would sell it to him for $355,000, because I'd bought it for $330,000 and had put probably $60,000 to $70,000 into land-scaping, fencing, a deck. But he said couldn't afford it right then.

I ended up carrying that house for nine months. We finally got an offer from someone for $350,000, but it was contingent on them selling their house, which they couldn't do. So I'm carrying this mortgage and paying rent in Buffalo. Then Presley calls me and says, "I'll buy it for $355,000." Turns out our real estate agents were working in the same office. I wanted to tell him to fuck off, but I also needed to sell the house.

Presley bought the house but ended up getting traded too. In September 1991 he went from the Hawks to the San Jose Sharks, and then in March of that same season he was traded again, from the Sharks to Buffalo. (In some ways, you could say he took my job—he was a right winger too—but I'd have been on my way out by then anyway.) But because of the high property taxes, he couldn't sell that house in Wheaton for years!

After my trade to Buffalo, the Sabres sent a guy everyone called "Shakey" to Chicago to get my car. Shakey was a part-time guy, friendly with the trainers. He mostly worked for the Rochester Americans, Buffalo's farm team. In Chicago, Joyce loaded the car with clothes for me so I'd have something decent to wear for the next few months. The car was that Mercedes, and when Shakey got it to Buffalo he drove to our practice rink. Mike Foligno saw that car and thought it must be management or a team doctor arriving. No one was very extravagant on that Sabres team.

When I finally saw my family again, it was the all-star break. The Sabres were in LA for our last game. Wayne Gretzky scored three against us, and we lost to the Kings, 5–3. I got shut out that night, but if I'd scored I'd have tied the Buffalo record for most consecutive games with a goal, at eight. After the game, I took the red-eye to Chicago, where the movers were loading up the truck. I got the family and we were off to Buffalo. By then I'd bought a house a few blocks away from my rental, but we couldn't get into it until the end of May, so we didn't unpack too many boxes.

In my final game as a Blackhawk, I scored the opening goal in a 7–2 win over Detroit at the Stadium. I scored a power-play goal in my first game with the Sabres, a 4–1 win (over Detroit again). I had those 25 points in 30 games in Chicago, and then, in 28 games with Buffalo, I had another 19 goals and 13 assists. Another 30-plus-goal season. I could still play.

And I thought I would play a lot in Buffalo, but that too would change.

12

SQUID, WHERE ARE YOU? (BUFFALO)

I will never forget the night of March 22, 1989.

We were playing the St. Louis Blues at the old Aud in Buffalo, our seventh-last game of the regular season, and we were leading 1–0 late in the first period. The Memorial Auditorium was one of those great old barns where the crowd felt like it was right on top of you. We were playing a pretty ordinary game, and it was noisy, as usual, but that quickly changed. Blues forward Steve Tuttle was going hard to the front of our net—a pretty normal play—but he got bumped and fell and his skate came up and caught our goalie, Clint Malarchuk, around the mask. At first we thought Clint had just gotten kicked in the mask, but then we saw the blood.

The skate sliced Clint's throat—sliced his carotid artery and partially sliced his jugular vein. My gawd, it was scary. There was blood squirting everywhere. And tons of blood on the ice—a huge puddle of it.

Jim Pizzutelli, who was our medical guy, our head trainer, probably saved Clint's life. He was a medic in the army, so he had seen some gruesome stuff. He was so calm when everything happened. He immediately jumped the boards, ran out onto the ice, grabbed Clint's throat with a bunch of gauze and squeezed hard. He asked Clint, "Can you get up? We don't have time to wait for a stretcher." Clint nodded. Jim took him off the ice and the doctors took over from there, taking him to the ambulance.

Back on the ice, there was a circle of blood that looked an inch thick and bigger than a manhole cover. Later, Clint told me he'd thought he was going to die. Apparently he had even asked for the team chaplain. I think we all probably thought the same. There was so much blood. All of us watching on the ice, we were scared silly. Joyce was in the stands, in the corner at that end of the rink, sitting near Clint's girlfriend. Two fans had heart attacks. We thought we were watching a man die.

We heard that in the ambulance Clint said to the doctor, "Can you get me back by the third period?" That was Clint. He later found out they needed about three hundred stitches to close the wound, which was half a foot long. It's amazing he lived—a tribute to him, our trainer and the doctors, with a little help from above, I would say.

For the rest of the game, it literally felt like we were playing shinny. Nobody went near anybody. We lost the game 2–1, but nobody cared. Afterwards, we were sitting in the dressing room and there was no word yet from the hospital. We didn't know if our goalie was alive. Finally, about an hour and half later, we were told that he was okay. Everyone went home then, still shaken, but relieved.

Clint was in hospital for only a few nights, and once he got out, he came to practice every day to watch and hang out. He seemed fine. Incredibly, Clint was back in goal for us just ten days later. Unbelievable. He played the final 5:28 of the last game of the season, against Quebec, stopping the one shot he faced. When the injury happened, there was a little less than two weeks left in the regular season. We went 4-2-0 down the stretch, and we were off to Boston to start a best-of-five playoff series.

Jacques Cloutier was our other goalie. He played after Clint got hurt, which I'm sure wasn't easy, and he was between the pipes until those final six minutes of the regular season. Jacques started the first game in Boston and we won 6–0. It was a great start, and I had a goal. But back then you played two nights in a row, had a day off, played two in a row, had a day off, and then played the fifth game if necessary. Well, in the second game, our coach, Ted Sator, decided to start Clint. Sator didn't think Jacques, who wasn't a big guy, could play two nights in a row. But you know what? It's the playoffs. You've got to do what you've got to do, and I think Jacques could have done it.

We were up 3–0 four minutes into the second period when the Bruins started skating through the crease, getting close to Clint, and he started losing it. Understandably, he was rattled. We ended up losing the game 5–3, and then we lost the next two in a row, 4–2 and 3–2, at home. The Bruins finished us off 4–1 at Boston. Cloutier played the final three games of the series, including two nights in a row. If we'd won that second game, we would have won the series.

I don't blame Clint. I blame Sator for putting him in there. It was only about two weeks after that horrible throat injury, and I don't think anyone is going to feel too good mentally after nearly dying on the ice. Later on, I read Clint's book, *A Matter of Inches: How I Survived in the Crease and Beyond*. Knowing the mental health issues he'd gone through since he was twelve years old, it made sense to me why he kind of lost it during the game. He admitted that it wasn't until the off-season that the gravity of everything he had gone through settled in.

Clint was a pretty regular guy, or he seemed to be. Maybe he was hiding what he was going through, his emotional issues. We had picked him up in a trade a few weeks earlier, on March 6. We sent defenceman Calle Johansson and a second-round pick to Washington for him, along with defenceman Grant Ledyard and a sixth-round pick.

The only thing I noticed about Clint, which I thought was strange, was that sometimes after practice he'd go up to the weight room and be there for four or five hours. For any one of us four or five hours was a lot of time, I thought, but for a goalie? Back then, anyway, goalies weren't typically the best athletes on the team, but Clint was always in great shape. I don't think anyone was really aware of what he was going through mentally and emotionally. Back then, no one talked openly about this stuff—not like we're encouraged to do now. Had he talked to someone about it, maybe he could have gotten help and been a better goalie, been in better shape mentally. At one point after the throat injury he was having anxiety and depression issues. He couldn't sleep, and he wound up mixing painkillers with booze and his heart stopped. Later in life, he shot himself in the head with a rifle but somehow lived.

Clint was a great guy, a great team guy. He saw me at my less-than-finest moments too. And many of those came in the air.

We were flying home one evening after an afternoon game in Boston. Clint was in the back seat of the plane next to the washroom, and I was in the seat in front of him. The pilot came on and announced that in about thirty minutes they were going to ask us to buckle up and stay in our seats because we were going to hit some bad weather. So of course, I'm freaking out.

Clint went to the washroom, and I'm sitting on the arm of his chair waiting for him to come out so that I could go in. Then, all of a sudden, the plane just dropped and it was like I flew up and hit the ceiling. I jumped into my seat. We were going through thunderstorms. We had to reroute and go out around Pittsburgh and Cleveland and back into Buffalo.

I honestly don't think there was anyone on that plane who thought we were going to make it. At first, there were a few guys who were like, "Yahoo, this is like a bronco ride!" After a few minutes, though, there was dead silence. The plane wasn't just going up and down, it was going sideways too. It was pretty bad. And there was no booze, no beers on the charters, and we weren't allowed to order on the commercial flights—although if you sat far enough back from the coaches and management you could usually sneak one or two.

There were flights when I was so scared I would actually scream. In Buffalo, Alexander Mogilny was an even worse flier than I was—and I didn't think that was possible! One time we were flying back from LA and stopped in Detroit to switch planes. When we all got to the other gate, Alex was nowhere to be seen. He'd bought a bus ticket to get the rest of the way to Buffalo. For the rest of the season, Shakey, the part-time guy who helped out in Rochester, drove him to road games.

When Alex did fly, I would sit with him. Somehow, that made me feel better. Maybe seeing him in worse shape than me was a distraction, or maybe it calmed me down. Or maybe misery really does love company. When I was with the Leafs, Bob McGill—Big Daddy—used to tell the story of a flight we'd been on from Winnipeg to St. Louis. During the trip the plane had a number of free falls—it felt like we were falling out of the sky. He said I was screaming so loud, for so long, that it actually made everyone else calmer because it became so comical.

If I was playing today—with the teams flying in the same aircraft, with the same pilots and crew for every flight, with the big A320 planes with first-class seats and good food—it would be a little easier. Those planes can handle the weather so much better than the small ones we used to fly, and the pilots are aware they have to make the flight as smooth and comfortable as possible, even if it means rerouting and taking a little longer to get to the destination. Commercial flights can't afford to do that, and small planes take a pounding.

I tried hypnosis, all kinds of things, but nothing ever made me feel more comfortable or relaxed. In the last few years I was playing I even went as far as to get some medication from the doctor that was supposed to relax you to a point where you're not worried or scared, but that didn't work for me either. Not even the beer helped.

That first year in Buffalo, I scored 19 goals in the 28 games after the trade from Chicago, but that's also when the injuries started to pile up and my neck started to get bad. We were playing Detroit, and I was in the centre ice area when I got hit. I fell into the boards, went down and tried to scoop the puck with my stick. Adam Graves, who was an honest player, was skating by and wasn't looking. His knee accidentally hit me on the side of the head and my neck twisted. I used to get burners down my arm, but after that hit it became burners down both arms. They lasted for days. My fingers were a little numb, and that kept happening. Finally, the doctors sat me. I think I was out for two weeks.

When I'd arrived in Buffalo, Lindy Ruff had my familiar number 22. I wore 12 instead. He was traded to the Rangers in March, so I grabbed my number and wore it for the rest of my time in Buffalo. Some other familiar parts of my life in Toronto caught up to me in Buffalo. Or in LA, to be specific. One night after a game against the Kings, I hit the showers. A minute later I hear this booming voice in the dressing room, "Squid! Squid, where are you? I've got plans for after the game." My new teammates were shocked that John Candy had just walked in; they were even more surprised that he knew me personally.

My first full season in Buffalo was okay, but again I had injuries. I still played 70 games and had 29 goals, but I was a lot more comfortable off the ice. We had settled into our house, my family was with me, life was back to normal. Justin was born that summer in Buffalo. I really enjoyed Buffalo. We lived in a town called Clarence, which was beautiful. The school system was excellent, I liked playing in the Aud, and we had a pretty good team. I got to play with Mogilny, who was a great talent. Christian Ruuttu was my centre when I first got there, and after that it was Pierre Turgeon, who was our leading scorer with 106 points.

Sator had been fired after the playoff loss to Boston, along with assistant coaches Barry Smith and Don Lever (briefly my teammate in Vancouver). They brought in Rick Dudley, who'd been a very popular Buffalo player, as head coach, and a young John Tortorella as an assistant. They were great. After Mike Keenan, Duds was probably the best coach I played for. He was well prepared. He and Torts watched a ton of video after practice. He'd have about twenty sheets of paper with all sorts of notes on the bench in front of him. That Buffalo team was very well coached.

There was a funny night early that season—maybe it was a hint that I'd have a future as a coach. We were playing in Toronto, and I noticed that Gary Leeman's number 11 had been circled on the starting lineup, but from the bench I could see that Vincent Damphousse, who wore 10, was on the ice instead. I told the coaches and the Leafs got called for a bench minor. Dave Andreychuk—a great teammate who sat beside me in the dressing room and always kept me smiling—scored on the power play and we went on to beat the Leafs 7–1. I even got a goal that night (Dave and Gary, who were both part of that sequence, would eventually be the other two players to score 50 goals for Toronto, Dave after he was traded from Buffalo).

We finished third overall behind Boston and Calgary with 45 wins and 98 points, and we got Montreal, which had 93 points, in the first round of the playoffs. Even with home-ice advantage, we lost in six games. We had gone into the series as the favourite, but that Montreal defence—especially Chris Chelios and Craig Ludwig—was so good. And they had Stéphane Richer, who scored 51 goals that season; Shayne Corson and Guy Carbonneau; and Patrick Roy in goal. It was a disappointing loss, but at least it was to a very good team. Despite the series loss, we were looking ahead to fall with a lot of optimism. We figured we were close to being good enough to win. Unfulfilled optimism seems to have been a constant in my career.

Prior to my third season in Buffalo, in June 1990, we acquired Dale Hawerchuk, who was a top talent, and a first-round pick (who turned out to be Brad May) from Winnipeg in exchange for Phil Housley, Scott Arniel, Jeff Parker and a first-round pick (who turned out to be Keith Tkachuk). Dale was a great addition. He probably needed a change of scenery after nine years with the same club, just as Housley needed to move on.

Dale led the Sabres that year in scoring, with 89 points. I was fifth, with 25 goals and 52 points in 71 games. That was a crazy season: we finished with a 31-30-19 record—yes, 19 ties. We were a better team than our record suggests, but our goaltending was an issue. Daren Puppa and Clint were basically splitting the games, with Darcy Wakaluk playing some, but the goaltending just wasn't good enough.

Not sure if it was the pressure in Buffalo or just his nature, but Duds had some bad moments. He ran a good bench, no question. But he lost it a lot. Duds would give it to the referees and linesmen all the time. Some nights he was relentless. And he didn't always pick the best time to do it. We talked to him about it, tried to explain that he wasn't doing us any favours, but he couldn't stop himself. The officials would even talk to us about it on the ice, telling us to get him to settle down.

One night the season before, for example, we were playing LA at home and were up 5–2 in the last minute. Duds had been riding the officials all night. The Kings rushed into our zone—our bench was right by our blue line—and they were probably three feet off-side. The linesman was Ron Asselstine, a veteran who worked a lot of big games, a good guy who everyone called Bear because he kind of looked like one out there. Ron put his arms out, indicating the play wasn't offside, and LA proceed to score. Ron turned around and looked at Duds and just smiled. That was his way of getting back at him for not backing off. Duds went nuts. He ripped the papers he had in his hand in half and started banging on the glass behind the bench, which would sway two or three feet, scaring the crap out of the people sitting on the other side. They started running out of the section, afraid the glass would collapse. It was quite comical. Bear knew we weren't going to lose the game, and he sent his message. Not that the coach got it.

Duds would lose it a lot between periods, too. One time he came in and was going nuts on us. We had those big Gatorade jugs on the table in the middle of the dressing room—one was full of water, one had Gatorade. He came in and slapped one over onto the floor. The cover came off and all the Gatorade spilled onto the Sabres logo on the carpet. The next game he did the same thing, slapped the jug onto the floor, but this time the cover didn't come off so he started kicking it, trying to knock the cover loose. There were some funny times like that, but we'd just drop our heads and bite our cheeks, or whatever it took not to laugh. Duds was one of those guys you didn't want to catch you laughing. He was a hard-nosed player. He played that way, coached that way. But all told he was a good coach.

It's funny how guys change. Torts, as an assistant coach—and a good one at that—said hardly anything. Then he becomes a head coach and turns into this wild guy, going nuts all the time, jawing with reporters (Larry Brooks of the *New York Post* was a favourite and frequent verbal sparring partner), trying to get into the other team's dressing room (which he did when he was coaching Vancouver, pissed at the Calgary Flames). He became this outspoken head coach, wearing his heart on his sleeve. And he's good at that job, too. Becoming an NHL head coach changes you in some ways, because there's a different pressure and you're the one who has to talk to the press every day. Maybe he got tired of some of the same questions, and some of the media really do push your buttons. But Torts was one of the quietest, nicest guys I ever had as an assistant coach.

That 1990–91 season, I managed to play 71 games, but I wasn't always feeling right. I scored 25 goals, as I mentioned, but I think I could have easily scored 35 if my health had been better. On Halloween, we were playing Boston. It was early in overtime and I got hit from behind by Bob Sweeney. I was going headfirst into the boards, but luckily I turned and hit my shoulder instead. Man, that hurt. I was lucky I didn't break my neck. I don't think Sweeney meant to hurt me, but it was one of those hits from behind that deserves a suspension. He got a two-minute boarding penalty.

I had X-rays taken and could see there was a half-inch separation in the shoulder. I said to the doctor, "That doesn't look very good," but the doc insisted it was an old injury. "What do you mean an old injury?" I asked. He said, "You've separated your shoulder before, right?" I told him I had—both shoulders, four or five times. He said, "Well, that's from one of the other injuries." If that was the case, I wondered, then why couldn't I move my arm? Something had happened when Sweeney hit me—it wasn't entirely some old shoulder separation. But the doctors kept telling the trainers and coaches that I was fine. I started playing after a week or so, but I had a tough time. I couldn't even hook somebody. I'd have to let go of my stick, the shoulder was so sore. I didn't play very well after that hit; I'll be the first to admit it. But that shoulder had a lot to do with it.

The following season, 1991–92, was a disaster. The Sabres hired John Muckler to be their director of hockey operations. I had a history with John—and not a good one—dating back to his days as an assistant coach with the Edmonton Oilers and 1984 Team Canada. As a player, Muckler had been a lifer in the old East Coast league and a teammate of my former coach John Brophy with the Long Island Ducks. In Edmonton, he'd been an assistant and then associate coach to Glen Sather through four Stanley Cup wins and head coach for the fifth in 1990. Dating back to the WHA days, he used to chirp me alongside Sather and I'd tell him to shut up. It seemed like he just didn't like me for some reason. I'd never really given a shit, but his arrival in Buffalo meant that might change.

It was widely believed that Muckler was going to take over from Gerry Meehan as the Sabres GM. Gerry had done a terrific job, bringing in the likes of Turgeon and Hawerchuk. He traded for me, too. And later he acquired Pat LaFontaine and Dominik Hašek, although I found out years later the Sabres actually put Hašek on waivers the same season in which they acquired him from Chicago. There was only one team that claimed him, though—the Hawks. And the league ruled that Chicago couldn't take him back in the same season. That worked out pretty well for Buffalo.

Muckler did take over as GM, but not formally until 1993. In that 1991–92 season, he started off helping Gerry, but it felt like

Muckler was running things, or at least had a lot of influence. Duds was fired after 28 games, and I believe it was Muckler who pushed for it. We were 9-15-4 and falling fast. I started the year playing with Turgeon as my centre, and after the first five games of the season, I had a goal and three assists. But then the drought set in and I started sitting. I went three more games without a point, sat three, played two more without a point, sat six, played two more without a point, sat four, played one more without a point, sat two. Then Duds was fired.

I was getting chances to score, but I couldn't get anything to go in. That's when you really start pressing—and sitting. My shoulder was still bugging me from that Sweeney hit the year before, too. Nothing was going right.

In Muckler's first game behind the bench, I didn't dress. I should have taken that as a sign. Later, we had a game in Montreal when he called up three or four guys from Rochester. A number of our regular guys were banged up. I dressed, I warmed up, and then I didn't get a shift the whole game. I had relatives there, because my father's sisters and other family lived in Montreal and the surrounding area. But they didn't see me play a single minute. Not one. I had never gone through anything like that in my entire career. I was as embarrassed as I was angry.

When we got back to Buffalo, I went in to see John and asked him why he'd embarrassed me like that.

"What do you mean, embarrass you?" he said.

"You dressed me. I've been in the league twelve years—this is my thirteenth season—and you don't play me one shift."

"I wasn't trying to embarrass you."

"Well, for not trying you did a pretty good job of it." He was indignant. "Why don't you move me? It's quite obvious you don't want me here."

"Nobody wants you," he said.

"Put me on waivers." Boston had lost Cam Neely to injury that year. He had played just nine games, and they needed a right winger who could score. Muckler said he'd already put me on waivers, but I knew it would have been recallable waivers—and no one was going to waste their time making a claim when they knew he'd just recall me. He tried to say otherwise, but we both knew recallable waivers wasn't the same. I asked him to put me on regular waivers and see what happened. He wouldn't do it. I went to Gerry and I asked him to talk to John, and maybe between the two of them they could find a team to send me to. If not, I told him to just send me to the farm team in Rochester at the trade deadline, so at least I could play. Ottawa and Tampa were coming into the league the next year, and they'd see I could still contribute.

After Muckler took over, I ended up playing seven more games, 20 in total of an 80-game season. The few times I did play only happened because we had injuries, and even then I got very limited ice time. As it turned out, my last NHL goal and point had come in the fifth game of the season—against Vancouver, ironically. What turned out to be my last NHL game was February 4, 1992, in Buffalo, a 7–3 victory over the Washington Capitals. I didn't have a point or a shot.

But I knew I wasn't finished. So I went to Rochester.

13

SILVER LININGS (ROCHESTER)

I hadn't gotten steady ice time in four months. Twenty appearances with Buffalo by early February, then nothing. Now in the AHL, Don Lever was my coach, Terry Martin was the assistant—both good guys—and I was playing a lot. It's amazing what a difference an hour's drive east can make in a hockey player's life.

With the Rochester Americans, I was getting some real ice time in the semifinals against the Adirondack Red Wings. We lost, but then they beat St. John's in the finals to win the Calder Cup. I got in a dozen regular-season games before the playoffs—scoring four goals and 13 points—and played in 16 post-season games, with four goals and eight points. The game was fun for me again.

In Buffalo, obviously, I'd been pissed off more than anything. Frustrated. I wasn't drinking every night, but I was drinking a lot more than before I started sitting so often. Getting drunk wasn't the smartest thing to do, I know, but I guess it took my mind off my frustrations. I didn't get into the hard stuff much, but six beer usually did the trick. That was a tough spell for me, no question.

On the road, when I knew I wasn't going to be playing or we would have a night off, I'd practise, skate my balls off after practice, and then go and get dinner and drink. A lot of times I'd drink by myself because the other guys were playing. If there was someone else who wasn't playing, well, they'd come along and have a few.

When you're not playing, you've got to do something to fill the time. When you're feeling shitty about yourself because you're not playing, the last thing you want to do is go to your room, sit alone and watch TV. And you don't want to bother your roommate if he's playing. Dale Hawerchuk was my roommate for a while. If I was in a bad mood, the last thing he needed was me hanging around and complaining about the way the team was treating me. So I'd go for dinner, go to a bar, have my beers and head back to the hotel, but not too late, to avoid waking him up. I'd be back by ten o'clock and then I'd fall asleep.

I kept it together on game days, even if I didn't think I was playing. Where I might otherwise go out for something to eat after practice, maybe have a beer, you never knew what might happen on a game day. Someone could get sick, and all of a sudden you've got to go in. I remember one night in Toronto, Billy Derlago got to the rink and was told he wasn't playing. He went across the street from Maple Leaf Gardens to Le Baron, a steakhouse we used to frequent. Billy had a couple of beers before dinner, a big steak and a glass of wine. He was on his second glass of wine when someone ran over from the rink and grabbed him. Someone had gotten hurt during warm-up. Billy had to race over, get dressed and play. He actually played pretty well. I think he had a couple of points—not just pints—that night and was one of the three stars of the game.

I never had anything like that happen to me. I'd always wait until the game was over, especially remembering that.

So, all in all, I wasn't happy in Buffalo—except for when I was at home with Joyce and the boys. Life always seemed better at home because of them. I lost my grandmother that year, though. That was really tough. There was a message on the home phone one day from my father. He said, "There's been a death in the family," and hung up. Didn't say who. I had no idea who died. My dad had taken her to the hospital with massive heart pain. She never came home. She was also suffering from dementia. My mother looked after her and Uncle Frank, feeding them three times a day, making sure they were okay. My grandmother was president of Cerebral Palsy PEI, obviously because of Frankie. My mom and dad were a huge part of her life. They helped keep her going, looking after her when she was failing and keeping Frankie out of an institution. John Allan Cameron, who was a wonderful man, would go to my grandmother's house and play for Frankie. That was special. When my grandmother passed, Frankie moved into my parents' home. My parents took Frank to concerts. They looked after him for a year and a half before he was finally moved into a very nice home. I went to the funeral, but couldn't stand to view the coffin. Funny thing, my dad was the same way.

We had a lot in common, my dad and me. He was an introvert, hated to lose control of anything. He didn't even like to sit in the stands when he came to see me play in Toronto. He'd just have a few beers in the Hot Stove Lounge with Greg Terrion's dad and watch the game on TV. I guess that fear of losing control was why he hated flying as much as I did.

My grandmother had taught me to look for the silver lining, and packing my gear and getting out of Buffalo helped me feel like I was finally regaining some control over my future. Rochester had put some of the fun back into hockey for me. I wasn't done.

After the playoffs, though, I was done with Buffalo. The Sabres bought me out of the last year of my contract for the next season. The buyout back then was two-thirds of your salary over twice the number of years. I received two-thirds of $350,000—roughly $110,000 times two years. Nice money, but I wasn't playing in the NHL.

The next year, 1992–93, the Ottawa Senators and Tampa Bay Lightning were coming into the league as expansion franchises. When the NHL was considering bids for teams, most people expected that Hamilton and St. Petersburg would be the new franchises. Hamilton's bid was backed by Ron Joyce, who was the head of Tim Hortons at the time, and St. Pete's was backed by Pete Karmanos of Compuware fame. They would have been strong ownership groups, but they balked at the finance terms the league had put in place. So Ottawa and Tampa got the nod. None of that mattered to me, of course. We players were all pretty much oblivious to what was going on in the boardrooms. All we cared about was that there were more roster spots.

I made a crucial mistake, though. I didn't get myself an agent and I should have. My long-time agent Bill Watters had taken a job in management with the Maple Leafs, and I didn't hire anyone. I had that deal with Buffalo and figured I could take care of things myself. I called both Phil Esposito, who was running Tampa, and Mel Bridgman, who was the GM in Ottawa, to see if

I could get a sniff. I called them both maybe eight or nine times and never heard back from either one. Finally, I reached out to Dale Hawerchuk, who was living near me in the Buffalo suburb of Clarence. John Ferguson Sr. was the director of player personnel with Ottawa, and Dale had played for him in Winnipeg. I asked Dale if he would call Fergie for me, which he did. Fergie called and I told him I just wanted to play. I said I would play for the minimum salary, we could build in some bonuses, but I just wanted to play. "I'm from Ottawa," I said. "It's where I was born, and I know I can still score 20 to 25 goals." My shoulder was feeling much better by then, too. Fergie couldn't believe I would play for the minimum, but I would have. I just wanted to keep playing. Fergie called Bridgman, and then called me back a few days later. He was pissed off because Bridgman didn't want to sign me. I appreciated Fergie trying. Anyway, the franchise under Bridgman turned out to be a bit of a tire fire.

So I ended up signing with Vancouver—back to where it all began for me in the NHL—but this time as a player–assistant coach with Hamilton, which was the Canucks' AHL farm team. The thinking was that if I played well in Hamilton, the Canucks could sign me to an NHL contract and bring me up during the season. That was my hope, too. But the first day of training camp, in Victoria, BC, we were doing a drill and one of the guys, who was supposed to be on the other side of the ice, crossed over to my side. I was looking for a pass and he hit me. I broke the scaphoid bone in my wrist. I was in a cast for fourteen weeks, and when the doctor took the cast off, he said I still needed surgery. I said, "No way, just make me a leather brace, because I'm done after this year." I'd already made up my mind. After everything that had happened over the past few years, it was time to move on. I ended up playing only 38 games that season, although I did have 16 goals and 31 points. Not bad numbers, all things considered.

At the end of the season, I started to get the same rash I'd occasionally had in Toronto and more often in Chicago. It came out of nowhere. It was so uncomfortable, I couldn't have played even if I'd been otherwise good to go, because I couldn't sleep. Once, it got so bad that I even ended up in hospital. My whole body was covered in it. It actually happened to quite a few players over the years. They nicknamed it "the gunk," and it could get bad enough to drive you out of the game. Gilles Gilbert, who I scored my third 50th goal against, had it bad. Tom Reid, a defenceman in Minnesota I played against, had to quit because of it. And, most famously, Marián Hossa, who won three Cups with Chicago, stopped playing in 2017 because of a skin condition that sure sounded like the gunk to me.

My neighbour in Buffalo was an allergist. He researched all the materials used in our equipment and all the chemicals that were used to treat or make the leather, foam, rubber, you name it. He'd put small doses in my arms to test for reactions. I was allergic to almost all the chemicals in my gear. My sweat would bring out the chemicals and they'd absorb into my body, and then I'd break out in this wild rash that would be on my sides, my butt, my legs, everywhere. I'd had the rash at times in Buffalo, too. I never realized until I finished playing why it hadn't been as much of a problem in Toronto. We had a sauna at the Gardens, and I'd go in there whenever I could. I was basically sweating the chemicals out.

These days, the rash doesn't bother me too bad when I play alumni games. If we play three games in three days, I might get a bit of it the next weekend, but when I'm not on the ice every single day, I don't have a problem, and obviously we're not sweating and exerting ourselves the way we did when we were in the NHL.

George McPhee, who is now the president of hockey operations with the Vegas Golden Knights, a really bright guy, was the GM in Hamilton. He worked for Pat Quinn in Vancouver. I called George, told him about the rash and said that I couldn't play anymore. I told him he could cut my pay if he wanted, because I wasn't playing, and just pay me to be an assistant coach. That would have been fine with me. But George said, "No, you did a good job for us. Just keep doing it and we'll pay you." George was really good about it. As an assistant coach, I didn't have much say. Jack McIlhargey was the coach and he called the shots, old-school coaching. But George keeping me on like that gave me a taste of what coaching was like, and one of my goals post-career was to get into coaching.

I was staying in Hamilton two or three nights a week. I had an apartment. Most of the time, I was going back to Buffalo, but if we had a game in Hamilton and a practice in the morning, or a game the next day, I would stay. That's when I'd go to the bar. It had been a really tough couple of years. All the crap in Buffalo, the injuries, not getting a chance with Ottawa and Tampa, and then all of a sudden the broken wrist and the rash. It was an ugly ending. I was only thirty-three years old and it was over. It hurt. All of your life, it's about playing the game you love, and then all of a sudden it's done. It's not easy, especially when it's not entirely on your terms. It's not how you want to leave. It sucks.

On top of knowing my career was over, I had to watch as the Leafs went on that amazing playoff run in the spring of 1993. I couldn't stop thinking about what could have been. Cliff Fletcher was GM. Pat Burns was the coach. With all due respect, in my time in Toronto we never had anyone close to the calibre of those two running the team. What would have happened if I'd somehow stayed in Toronto? I watched it all unfold: winning the first two rounds, going to Game 7 in the conference final. If I'd just stayed in Toronto, I might have played a few more years. I was happy for the Leafs, but that was hard to watch.

14

BEHIND THE BENCH
(CHARLESTON, SAINT JOHN)

So, I'm thirty-three years old in the spring of 1993, and suddenly I'm retired. My playing career is over, just like that. What happened next... well, let's just say I was fortunate, because it probably saved me from disaster.

If I'd had to sit around for a while, sorting out my next steps and brooding about what might have been, it could have gone bad. Really bad. Spending the next year or two sitting around missing the game, missing being around the rink and the guys, wondering every day what the hell I'm going to do with myself... the drinking would have gotten a lot worse.

But I got lucky.

I got a coaching job in Charleston, South Carolina. At least with coaching, you're still involved with the game, you're still at the rink every day. The difference is you have the futures of twenty or so young men in your hands. Staying in hockey and having that responsibility was a saving grace.

Charleston was a new franchise in the East Coast Hockey League, and the team had been named the South Carolina Stingrays. When I heard they were coming into the league, I got in touch with John Brophy, who was now coaching the Hampton Roads Admirals. Broph told me to get in touch with Pat Kelly, who was commissioner of the ECHL. Broph knew him well. Pat put me in touch with Frank Milne, who was the general manager in Charleston. I made the quick drive across the border to interview with Frank in St. Catharines, Ontario, where years ago he'd coached the junior team. I was pretty confident that with the knowledge I had gained over the years as a player and the various things I'd learned from my coaches along the way—good ideas and bad ones—I could do the job. Frank agreed, and I became the first-ever coach of the new Charleston ECHL team.

It was exciting. A new home, a new job, a new beginning. The team was part-owned by Frank, a Canadian investor named Joe Scanlon, and the great former hockey player Marcel Dionne, who had played for Frank as a junior in St. Catharines. Marcel eventually took over for Joe as president and CEO of the franchise, but after a while the ownership situation got too messy and they were forced to sell to local interests. Anyway, the Stingrays—who were originally supposed to be called the Sharks until someone realized San Jose might not like that—became the first hockey franchise in South Carolina.

Joyce, the kids and I moved to Charleston in August. After a week or so, I said to her, "I don't know if I can live here." It was so hot and humid. But I got used to it. We were also living in a hotel for a month or so, and the first pay took a long time to arrive. But

Charleston was beautiful, with a historic and charming downtown and great beaches. We eventually settled in Mount Pleasant, only a four-minute drive to the waterfront, and there were lots of golf courses (both features would prove helpful when I started recruiting players). The first thing I told management when I arrived was that I needed sixteen tickets for every game. I would take those tickets to four of the local golf courses and I'd give four to the pro at each course. Either they'd come to see us play and start talking about us, or they'd give them out to members. It also got us free golf at pretty much every course in the area.

I started reading books about psychology. Before we moved south, I went to a bookstore, bought five of them—three specifically on sports psychology—and I devoured them. They were incredibly helpful. I learned how to read people very quickly, how to get to know them quickly, even how to read facial expressions. It helped me understand what my players needed from me, whether I had to pat them on the back or kick them in the butt to get them going, or sometimes whether I wanted them on my team at all.

We started camp with only eight players, and there were a few times when Joyce and I wondered what we'd gotten ourselves into. Charlestown wasn't exactly a hockey town. At the start of the season, fans booed every whistle and gave the goalies standing ovations just for making a save. More than a few were asking when halftime was. Between the fans not understanding the game and the team being cobbled together at the last minute, it could be frustrating some nights. I had to learn to control myself on the bench. As a coach, I could fix things between periods or at practice, but during the game I couldn't control what was happening on the ice. After so many years as a player, that took some getting used to. I had a very helpful meeting with Andy Van Hellemond, who had been a great referee in the NHL and was overseeing the officials in the ECHL. He told me, "You can't be screaming at the players and the officials all the time, but when you do, keep your hands in your pockets, don't be waving your arms, at least look like you're in control." Andy helped me a lot.

One of the toughest parts of adjusting to coaching was dealing with the expectations I had for a player. Not everyone has the same skill level, or skill set. And not everyone can do the things I did as a player. I read that Wayne Gretzky had problems with that when he was coaching in Arizona. Obviously, his skills were otherworldly, but it's basically the same problem. Wayne had trouble at first understanding why his Coyotes players couldn't do things on the ice that had come so naturally to him. The answer is really quite simple: not everyone has your talent or ability. I learned that right away.

I couldn't expect everyone to do what I could do, but I could expect them to give 100 percent to whatever they were doing. And whatever role they played, I realized I had to make the player believe it was a big part of helping the team win. So, if a guy was the tenth forward, used sparingly, killing penalties, I needed to make him feel that what he was doing was just as important as the guy scoring goals on our number-one line. It's a message so many coaches have delivered, or tried to, over the years. It's what Broph tried to tell his players—even if sometimes he was misunderstood—and it works.

Communication, I discovered, was a big thing. I felt like I was able to communicate with the players on their level. I would pick three guys every day and would have a conversation with them. We talked on the ice before practice and in the office after practice. Sometimes it didn't even have anything to do with hockey—just "How's everything, is your girlfriend happy," that sort of thing. Even a simple conversation leaves the other person feeling good about themselves, feeling that you care about more than just their statistics. As a player, I always found that when a guy was comfortable and happy with his environment and the coach made him feel important, it made him feel better. In my case, at least, it made me play better, too.

The first year, we finished with a 33-26-3-6 record and made the playoffs, but we lost to Broph and Hampton Roads in the first round. Despite the loss, we were a first-year success story. The building was brand new, beautiful, in North Charleston, and it held just over ten thousand. We nearly filled it, night after night, averaging just over 9,100 fans a game. That was the most in the ECHL. I really enjoyed my first year of coaching. We loved living in South Carolina, the franchise was exciting, and I thought I had adjusted pretty well to hanging up my skates. But the season had one more lesson to teach the new coach.

Our final game was in Norfolk, which is not far from Virginia Beach and home to one of the largest US naval bases. The hotel we were staying in was located in, well, a not-so-great area. After we lost that night, the team bus went back to the hotel and I told the guys not to go out. I had the team credit card, so I offered to buy everyone a few beers at the hotel bar.

I ended up having a couple myself, then a couple more. Next thing you know, I'm in one of the players' rooms with a bunch of the guys. They had all kinds of booze, so they'd obviously never intended to leave the hotel. We're in the room and having a few more drinks—and the next thing I remember is waking up in my hotel room.

I want to back up a few months. As nice as our new city was, life in Charleston hadn't been easy. In January, Joyce was diagnosed with clinical depression. It was a tough time for her. Assenta, the dog she'd had for fifteen years, needed to be put down; she'd had that old German shepherd nearly as long as she'd had me. It was a culture shock, too, being in a southern town after growing up in PEI and living in all those northern cities: Toronto, Chicago, Buffalo. And I hadn't been the easiest of companions either. I'd gotten drunk at a golf outing during the season and passed out at the course. Joyce was embarrassed—too embarrassed to continue going on like that, especially dealing with her depression. So I went to see a doctor about it. He thought I needed to go to rehab, which would mean quitting the team. In the midst of this, the doctor found a deeper issue.

For years, I'd been self-medicating to cope with undiagnosed anxiety. Knowing that helped explain the terror I felt on airplanes, and the discomfort in cars I wasn't driving, or in any other situation I couldn't control—even behind the bench, when I could no longer jump on the ice and score a much-needed goal to turn a game around. In Buffalo, there had been a few flare-ups when my heart was racing and I thought I was having a heart attack. Some neighbours helped get me to the hospital. I'd lost years of sleep to runaway anxiety. Looking back, it's kind of surprising that I'd ever been able to play at all. The doctor helped me find the right medication to treat the anxiety, but by the time we hit the hotel bar in Norfolk after that lost playoff series, I still hadn't kicked the habit of my other medicine.

I don't remember how I got to my hotel room. I woke up with no memory of leaving the players' room or anything that happened after that. That's not a good feeling. I decided, for the first time, to quit drinking. I was turning thirty-five in May, was married with two kids, and I decided that was it. I didn't drink again for about fifteen years. It wasn't easy at first, especially when the next season got underway. You're with the guys, you're out for dinner together, days off. But the longer I went without drinking, the easier it got.

The team was affiliated with Buffalo, with their farm team in Rochester and, to a lesser degree, with Toronto. Bill Watters, who had been my agent, was now assistant GM in Toronto. So I would go to Rochester's camp, then to Newmarket (where the Leafs' farm team was located), and spend a couple of weeks looking at the players, watching the guys they brought in on tryouts for the AHL teams who didn't make the cut. I tried to talk those guys into coming down to Charleston. I couldn't offer a lot of money. On average, the best players were probably making $7,000, maybe $8,000. Rookies were making $250 a week. Mind you, we supplied the apartments and all the utilities, so they didn't have to live on those salaries alone.

In our second season, we finished first in our division and set a league record with 18 straight home wins, but we lost in the second round of the playoffs. In 1995, I doubled my duties, adding director of hockey operations to my head coaching duties. Then, in 1996–97, our fourth season in the league, we had a welcome addition to our coaching staff that made life away from the rink a little easier for me. Rick Adduono, who I had played with for a year in Birmingham and who'd helped me with scouting juniors in the Thunder Bay area, came down to Charleston and became an assistant coach. When the Stingrays were on the road, our radio broadcaster, our trainer, Rick and I—we'd all four go bowling in the evenings, just to pass the time. I even got my own bowling ball and shoes. Rick and the others might have a few drinks, but I'd just bowl and drink my ginger ale. Staying out of the bars helped me stay dry, and those guys were good company and never tempted me to pick up a drink.

Good things come in threes, and that year we were the best team during the regular season—we had a record of 45-15-0-10—and won the Kelly Cup as ECHL champions. The South Carolina Stingrays were the first team to accomplish both in the same year. In the Kelly Cup finals, we played the Louisiana IceGators. Doug Shedden, a former NHLer, was their coach. They were a pretty undisciplined team, and we won the series four games to one. Our power play was lights out, working at something like 38 percent efficiency—a crazy-good number. When they took penalties, which they did a lot, we capitalized.

That championship was an impressive accomplishment for a few reasons. In the second-last game of the regular season, winger Ed Courtney, who led our team in scoring with 54 goals and 110 points (he was second in the league in scoring), two-handed a guy in the face and got suspended for the entire playoffs. That was a big loss to our offence. Luckily, we still had some firepower. Mike Ross, a centre, had scored 50 goals and also had 110 points, and we'd made a couple of changes earlier that helped, including picking up a young guy, a little defenceman named Brad Dexter, who handled the puck really well, worked his tail off down low and was the quarterback on our power play.

To win a championship, you need not only skill but character. When Ed got suspended, guys stepped up and played hard every night. Our captain, Brett Marietti, who was from Haileybury, Ontario, wasn't the most skilled guy around, but he was good enough to be an offensive threat. Plus he had a big heart, could get physical and throw them—whatever we needed to win—and he led by example. Another key guy for us was Chris Hynnes, a defenceman from Thunder Bay. He was fearless while blocking shots. And a big part of that championship team was Jason Cipolla, a centre from Toronto who had spent some time with the St. John's Maple Leafs and scored well over a point per game for us that spring. Jared Bednar, who went on to coach the Colorado Avalanche, was a big part of our championship team, a rock-solid defenceman.

Even outside of that championship team, we saw some good players over my five years in Charleston. I coached Martin Biron, who had a very good career in goal with the Buffalo Sabres. My last year, I had Ryan Sittler, Darryl's son, for 44 games. And we had one other player none of us will soon forget—Mark Bavis.

Mark was a hard-working left winger who spent two seasons with us, from 1994 through 1996. He had played four years at Boston University and was a ninth-round pick of the New York

Rangers in 1989. In the 1995–96 season, he split the year between us and the Providence Bruins. After his career, Mark got into scouting and worked for the Los Angeles Kings. On September 11, 2001, Mark—thirty-one at the time—and the Kings' director of pro scouting, Garnet "Ace" Bailey, were both killed when their flight to Los Angeles, United Airlines Flight 175, was hijacked by terrorists and crashed into one of the World Trade Center towers.

Mark's number 12 was retired by the Stingrays, and I had the honour of being inducted into the club's hall of fame alongside his posthumous induction in 2003.

With that 1996–97 championship team—as with most minor league teams—the guys didn't make much money, so I asked our owner, a local guy named Jerry Zucker who bought the Hudson's Bay department store chain in Canada years later, if he was willing to pay them bonuses in the playoffs. He agreed. It wasn't a ton of money; everyone got somewhere in the $2,000 range. As it turned out, he paid some of the money and I paid $19,000 out of my own pocket to honour the promise we'd made to the players. Technically, the bonus wasn't something we were allowed to do, but the guys deserved it and there were teams paying out a lot more money under the table than we did that time.

Somehow, though, the ECHL found out about it, and they decided we'd broken salary-cap rules. The team was fined $50,000, and I was suspended for the first six games of the next season. But to me it was money well spent and, like I said, every team was doing something to help their guys. Maybe they weren't as good as NHLers and didn't draw the same kind of crowds or corporate sponsorships. But they put themselves and their families, if they had them, through a lot so the league could put on some very good hockey games. I respected that about the guys playing in the ECHL.

I loved coaching. I loved where my family was living. Joyce was very happy, especially since I'd stopped drinking. I had good people around me. And, obviously, we had a pretty good run. Jerry and his wife, Anita, were fantastic to work for. I was only thirty-four when I got into coaching, but the goal was to move up the ladder, hopefully to the highest level. And yet there I was, quite happy in Charleston. I wanted to stay.

After my fifth season, John Marks, who had been coaching in Charlotte, North Carolina, left to go to Greenville, where his five-year deal started at $120,000 a year, with an increase each year, and included a country club membership. In the five years John and I coached against each other, we pretty much had identical records and we both won a championship. So in the spring of 1998 I went to Jerry and told him I wanted to sign a ten-year deal. I said I wouldn't leave to go to the AHL. I'd leave only if an NHL job opened up. I wanted to start at $80,000 and go up by $5,000 each year, so by the end of my ten years I'd be at $125,000. There were bonuses, but the maximum bonus I could earn in a season, if we won everything and finished first overall, was maybe $30,000. Then 5 percent of whatever I made in bonuses would get added on to each additional year of the contract. He said no, that it was too much money. I had one more year left on my contract. I could have stayed, because we still had a good team, but I knew I'd be selling myself short. I thought I was being fair, so Jerry's answer really disappointed me. It wasn't going to happen.

I got lucky again on the coaching front. Soon after I decided to leave Charleston, the head coaching position with Calgary's farm team in Saint John, New Brunswick, became available. I interviewed with Al Coates, who was the Flames GM, and Nick Polano, who was GM of the farm team, and I got the job. So Nick became my new boss—and I soon discovered he was not a fun guy to work with.

We had a young team in the two years I was in Saint John. Back then, the AHL allowed you to dress sixteen skaters and two goalies unless the coaches on both teams agreed to dress seventeen or eighteen skaters, which I thought was a stupid rule. Just settle on a number and leave it, but don't put it in the hands of coaches to decide how many players to dress. I remember Michel Therrien was coaching in Fredericton, which was the Canadiens' farm team, and he would never dress more than sixteen skaters. He'd say, "I don't have extra players," but then I'd see six guys sitting in the stands. We had better depth, so he intentionally shortened the lineups. We got in a big argument over it before one game and almost came to blows.

But the more frustrating part of this was the phone call I'd get from Nick asking why a certain player, one of the young guys, hadn't played that night. I'd tell him: I can only dress sixteen skaters most games. I've got all these young guys, but I can't play them all. I need to put some other guys in the lineup so we at least have a chance to win. There has to be a balance. You want the young guys to get experience, but also to experience what it's like to win. Eventually, he told me he wanted a written report faxed to him after every game. I had to do that for about a year and half. It was a pain, but I did it. The stupid thing is that after almost every game

I was sending him almost the same report on every player, because they all played pretty much the same way from game to game. But Nick wanted a grade, so he got one.

I got other frustrating calls from Calgary, too. When Brian Sutter, who was coaching the NHL Flames, or Al Coates called to say they needed a player to fill a hole in the big team's lineup, they hardly ever called up the player I recommended. I'd tell them who I thought deserved to go to Calgary, and the next day I'd walk into the dressing room and the trainer would be packing someone else's bag. I think they only called up a guy I suggested once in two years. That was Chris Clark, halfway through my second year. And he ended up having a pretty decent NHL career.

After my second season, Al and Nick both got fired. We had meetings in Calgary with the development and scouting staffs, going over the depth chart for the entire organization. At the bottom of the rankings list they had Martin St. Louis, who was our best player in Saint John by a country mile. That year, he played 56 games with Calgary and had three goals and 18 points. He mostly played on the fourth line, but I knew he was better than that. I asked why they had him ranked so low. Tod Button, who was a scout with the Flames, started arguing with me, saying Marty couldn't play in the NHL. I asked him how many times he had seen Marty play. Tod said it didn't matter; he can't play in the NHL. I said, "Well, I think he can."

Marty was small, just five foot eight, which is probably why he wasn't drafted when he came out of the University of Vermont after a great college career. To Al Coates's credit, he signed Marty after he saw him play in the International Hockey League. My first year coaching Saint John, Marty had 62 points in 53 games; the next year he had 26 points in 17 games. I felt if Calgary put him with the right players, he'd score. He was strong enough and quick enough to get away from much larger opponents. I could see him being a 30-goal, 30-assist guy.

I thought they were overlooking another guy, too. Goalie coach Jon Elkin would let Jean-Sébastian Gigèure off the hook on almost every goal he allowed. They would go over the film together in my office, and all I kept hearing was, "That wasn't your fault, Giggy, that wasn't your fault." After a while I said, "Jonny, show me those goals that you said weren't his fault." I remember one example: there was a turnover in the neutral zone, but they scored from the hash mark by the boards, a wrist shot, short side over his shoulder. I said, "I don't give a shit if there were ten turnovers—he can't allow a goal from there on the short side." I told Jon, "If you don't start making him more accountable, make him work a little harder in practice, you're going to lose your job." Sure enough, halfway through my second year, they got rid of Jon. I told management to get Giggy a good goalie coach, one who would make him work harder and make him accountable. Do that, I said, and he'll be good.

In early June of 2000, Craig Button, Tod's brother, was hired as GM of the Flames. Coates had picked up the option on St. Louis's contract before he got fired, but Craig bought Marty out, let him go for nothing after he went unclaimed in the Columbus-Minnesota expansion draft. Marty was signed by Tampa Bay and went on to win two league scoring titles, a Hart Trophy as most valuable player, a Stanley Cup, Olympic gold—the list goes on—before being inducted into the Hockey Hall of Fame. And it was Marty who scored in double overtime in Calgary in Game 6 of the 2004 Stanley Cup final to send the series back to Tampa, where they ultimately won. I guess he could play, although I never dreamed he would one day do all that.

Craig traded Gigèure to Anaheim shortly after becoming GM. Giggy played a grand total of 22 games with the Flames in the two years I was in the organization. In Anaheim, with François Allaire as his goalie coach, Giggy won a Conn Smythe Trophy in 2003, despite being on the losing team, and in 2007, he led the Ducks to a Stanley Cup victory. The Flames got a second-round pick, who turned out to be Matt Pettinger, in exchange for him.

But Tod thought he knew a lot more than I did. For two years, I spent a lot of time with those two players. I knew what they could and couldn't do, but he didn't want to listen to me.

As I said, Craig was hired in early June, but league rules forbade him from taking part in the draft because he'd been working so recently with Dallas. The draft was in Calgary that year, right after the expansion draft, and we were all flown out for it. We were there for five, six days, meeting with the scouting staff. We'd go out for dinner and I sat beside Craig a couple of times, and we had great conversations.

After the draft, I went back to Saint John and got a call from Larry Carrière, who was the GM in Rochester. He needed a coach and wanted me to apply. I told him I had been treated pretty well by the Flames, and I was pretty sure my job was safe in Saint John, or maybe there might even be something in Calgary eventually. He kept insisting that I apply, which typically means that if you do apply you'll get the job. I didn't apply.

Then, in the middle of July, Craig called me and said the Flames were going in a different direction. I said, "Craig, it's the middle of July. Why didn't you tell me when I was in Calgary at the draft and I could have tried to find another job?" He said he didn't know in June who they were going to hire. They ended up hiring Jim Playfair, who I had played with in Chicago. I went to the press conference when they announced the hiring because I was still living in Saint John. I certainly didn't have any hard feelings against Jim. I was happy for him. I stuck around after the press conference and asked him when he got hired. He said, "Well, Craig was hired June 6, so it was probably a week, maybe a week and a half after that." I was so pissed off. I never said anything to Craig; I didn't think it was worth it. But that was a different story from the one he told me on the phone. To let me go at that time of the summer, when there weren't any jobs available—that was a lousy thing to do.

15

A CHERRY ON TOP (MISSISSAUGA)

During my seven-plus years with the Maple Leafs, playing for loose-cannon owner Harold Ballard, there were some very long seasons. Long, losing seasons. And all that losing and chaos behind the scenes was painful, despite any individual success. Losing sucks, and a hockey player will always trade personal gain to win, especially the Stanley Cup.

As tough as those Leafs seasons were, I'd always figured the good news was it couldn't possibly get any worse, right? Well, apparently it could. Because nothing compared to the 2000–01 season when I coached the junior Mississauga IceDogs of the OHL. Now that was a long, losing season.

It had been a tough summer. I had gone into the off-season thinking everything was fine with the Flames, that I'd done a pretty good job with a young team. The new GM had other ideas. I get it—changes happen. But his timing had cost me the opportunity to go after a coaching job with Rochester. And that left me looking toward the coming season with no plan and nothing to do.

Trevor Whiffen, a lawyer by trade, was the general manager of the IceDogs at the time. He'd also been my agent when I got into coaching. Trevor called me that summer and started talking about the junior team he was running, just west of Toronto. He asked if I would consider the coaching job. I wasn't sure. I had concerns. One was that in the IceDogs' first two seasons as an expansion team, they won a total of 13 games and went through three coaches (and a fourth who would stay on as an assistant).

The other concern was that Don Cherry was a part owner of the team—a strong personality and presence, to say the least. I had to think Don was interfering with those fired coaches, and I did hear whispers that he was heavily involved. I turned Trevor down a couple of times, but he kept calling. Finally, I thought, *Okay, I've heard a lot of rumours, a lot of speculation. I'll make my own judgments and see how it goes.* I did make a key stipulation, though: I told Trevor that I had to have a say in all transactions—drafts, trades, releases, everything. If I got that and the right amount of money, I'd take the job. I thought that might protect me from whatever had happened to the first three coaches.

The team agreed to my terms, and in late July I signed a two-year contract and moved Joyce and the boys to Oakville. I still had concerns, but at least I had a coaching job.

The headaches began soon after.

I think it was during training camp. I was in a hotel room with Don, Trevor and Bobby Orr, who was there because he was the agent for Jason Spezza, the captain of the team. Jason was only seventeen at the time, a six-foot-two centre who was tabbed to possibly go first overall in the NHL draft (he ended up going second overall to Ottawa). He was the number-one bantam pick, and he'd played with the OHL's Brampton Battalion as a fifteen-year-old before coming to Mississauga. In his first season with the IceDogs, Jason was second on the team in scoring, with 24 goals and 61 points in 52 games. He was also minus-49, but there were a lot of big minus numbers on that team, which went 9-56-1-2. Who could have imagined how good that would look compared to the season ahead?

The conversation turned to Jason and that I might have trouble with my captain because he didn't like to play defence. That caught me off guard. "If that's the case," I asked, "why did you make him captain?" Well, he was a hometown, star-calibre player you could build a team around. It made more sense to try to fix his flaws than to trade him. Hopefully, I could get through to him. I always looked at things positively and thought, *Let's just give it a try*. New coach, maybe new results. I still don't think he was lazy, he just didn't want to do certain things.

We were okay at the start of the season, although it was clear we had some deficiencies as a team. Six or seven games in, I wasn't happy with how Jason was playing. I don't know if he didn't want to play defence in his own zone as a centreman or he wasn't able to, but I couldn't get through to him. He was leaving the zone early, and I couldn't get him to do what I needed from him in our end. He didn't want to play defence. Defence is hard work. You don't have to be a superstar to play good defence, but you have to be positionally sound and relentless in your coverage. So I sat him out for the second period of a game in Sarnia, the eleventh game of the season. I put him back out in the third period and he was the best player on the ice, bar none. I'm thinking, *Maybe it worked. Maybe I got through to him.*

Fast-forward to our fifteenth game. We were in Kingston, and after a 2-4-2 start to the season, the losses were starting to mount. We'd lost six straight heading into that game. We had a pretty good first line with Jason, Brian McGrattan on right wing and Chad Wiseman on the left side. We were trailing big after two periods, and that line had been on for most of the goals against—a lot of which were caused by forwards not playing defence. I would have McGrattan play down low, and I told Jason to cover the left point. He wouldn't do it. So I benched the line for the entire third period. When we got a power play with about three minutes left in the game, Jason started heading over the boards.

"Where do you think you're going?" I said.

He looked at me and said, "We've got a power play." I said, "Yes, but I'm not putting you on the ice to maybe get yourself a point after the way your line played." I felt bad because he was so talented; he was one helluva player. But if we were going to be successful, we needed him to get back and play in his own zone. Not just him, everybody. The day after that game, which we lost 7–3, he demanded a trade. The media reported it on November 7. Both he and Bobby wanted him out, so I knew it was going to happen.

Depending on the source, Jason was either not getting along with me (naturally, he wouldn't have been happy with the benching) or he was tired of Don and all the losing. He was a good kid, pretty quiet. I never had a problem with him as a person. He was never disrespectful and never gave me any trouble—except for the fact that he wouldn't do what I asked him to do. All Jason ever said publicly was that things weren't going well, and it was time for a change.

I talked to Trevor, Elliott Kerr (a part owner) and Don, and told them that while we were waiting to make a trade—which we needed to do pretty quickly—we couldn't have Jason around the team. It was going to be a zoo. The media were going to catch on to his demand, and having an unhappy captain around wasn't going to be good for the team, or for Jason himself. We made a collective decision that we would send him home and try to make the trade as quickly as possible. After practice, I had a talk with Jason. I explained the situation and the plan to him, and he was okay with it. He went into the dressing room, packed up his stuff, hung out with his teammates for a little bit, and then he left.

The next thing you know, I get a phone call from Don. He says, "What the hell did you do to Spezza?" I asked him what he was talking about. He told me Bobby had called him and said I wouldn't let Jason in the room or talk to his teammates. I told Don that I'd had a talk with him, that he was okay, and that he'd packed his stuff and had a chance to say goodbye to his teammates. But Don said, "That's not what Bobby told me." I said, "You better talk to Bobby and Darren Ferris [Jason's other agent] again and have them talk to Jason, because that's exactly what happened."

That was the beginning of the end for Don and me.

Jason was willing to be traded to six teams, and I think his preference was Brampton because he'd played for them and coach Stan Butler when he was fifteen. It was also close to home (Jason is from Toronto). But Brampton wasn't making a good enough offer for us to trade him to a team we'd be playing frequently and hearing about in the Toronto media. As I recall, Erie made a late offer, but it came down to two teams: Sarnia and Windsor.

I had watched both teams play a couple of times. To my mind, the Sarnia deal was much better, especially if they were willing to include seventeen-year-old Eric Himelfarb, who was a good little centre. I thought their offer would instantly make us a better team. Windsor was offering four guys and a couple of draft picks, but I didn't think it was nearly as good a package as the three guys we'd be getting from Sarnia.

We had a meeting—remember, in my contract I'd asked for input into all transactions, and this was a big one—and we decided to make the deal with Sarnia. At least that's what I thought when I left the rink. When I came to work the next day, I was told the trade was done. I asked when the Sarnia guys were arriving. Turns out, never. They made the deal with Windsor. Our head scout, who was a good friend of Don's, lived just outside Windsor, and I still wonder if that was a factor in the change of heart.

I was so pissed off. Like I said, having input was a part of my contract. A big part. It wasn't that I had to make all of the decisions, but I had to at least be involved in them. As far as I was concerned, we had agreed we were doing the Sarnia deal. As it turned out, of the four players we got from Windsor, two really weren't good enough to play in the OHL. Yes, they could play on our team, but not most teams. On top of that, one was from Windsor, and he got homesick and went back.

Trevor is a great lawyer, a really good person, and we're still friends today. But he was inexperienced as a GM, and there was the Don factor. I still wonder if Trevor had been overruled.

When you're trading a player of Jason Spezza's calibre, it's very difficult, if not impossible, to win the trade. You know you're giving up the best player in the deal, or at least the best at that time. But I thought we could have done better with Sarnia. To put it in perspective, when we dealt Spezza, he had seven goals and 30 points—as many as the four players we acquired combined.

More importantly, things weren't going great off the ice either. While the situation with the IceDogs was starting to unravel, our house in Oakville burned down!

It was Halloween night and I was watching our farm team, the tier-2 Mississauga Chargers, play. My older son, Jeff, thought his hockey practice was still on, so Joyce dropped him off at the rink. My youngest, Justin, was trick-or-treating with his buddies. Because it was Halloween, Jeff didn't have a practice. He waited for a while, no one showed up, so he called home to get a ride. When Justin got back he set his bag on the kitchen table—a big wooden table with a big candle on it, five candles in one. Joyce rushed Justin and our German shepherd into the car and off they went to pick up Jeff. The bag must have fallen over and banged into the candle. Whatever happened, when they got back the house was engulfed in flames. Our house burned down, or at least most of it.

I'm thinking, *What's going to go wrong next?* I'm dealing with all that—our house in ruins—at the same time I'm dealing with Don (who barely said a word to me about the fire) when our captain is about to ask for a trade and we can't win a hockey game.

Needless to say, our season didn't improve—not by a long shot. After that fateful Kingston game, we lost five in a row, in the midst of a 12-game losing streak, and wound up going winless in 25!

We also started to pile up some key injuries—to guys such as McGrattan, who halfway through the year had 20 goals. He blew out his knee. We were just a terrible team. Some nights our goaltending could hold us in for a while, but it was a rough go. The kids were great, really great, but they just weren't good enough.

Just before Christmas, Don came into my office. We had a defenceman we'd picked up from Kitchener. He was really slow, couldn't play at that level, but Don liked him because every time he got the puck he shot it out off the glass. You know how, on TV, he always applauded guys who did that? Well, he meant it. Don told me he wanted me to play this guy.

"Are you asking me or are you telling me?" I said.

He thought for a minute. "I'm telling you."

So I played the guy for three games, played him regularly, and he was minus-16 or -17. Forwards were going around him like he was standing still. I didn't play him after that and never heard another word from Don about it.

Of course, Don had plenty to say about other things. Shortly after the fiasco with the defenceman, Don started leaving messages on my office answering machine. He would watch the game, go home, probably have a few "pops," as he liked to call beer to keep his TV segment family friendly, and then he'd leave me a message. And they weren't nice messages.

I always came in to the office in the morning to watch the game tape from the night before. This one time, after a loss, there was a message on my machine from Don: "Well, that was quite a loss last night. You couldn't coach a good fucking peewee team." That's exactly what he said. It was probably the tenth time he'd left a message along those lines, but this one was the strongest.

I called Don and said I really thought we needed to talk. He agreed, so we decided to meet two days later in the morning, around ten or eleven o'clock at the latest, before everyone else arrived at the rink. Well, he ended up walking in about one in the afternoon, when everyone was there.

"I'm here!" he yelled out. I asked everyone to leave the office. I asked him to close the door and he didn't do anything. I said, "Close the goddamn door." He did, and we had it out.

"You're being an asshole, leaving those messages," I told him. I went off on him.

And he says, "I can see you don't want to win."

"What the hell are you talking about? I'm trying to win, but we're not good enough, and our best player asked to be traded. We've got to be patient. Hopefully we can move some older guys for younger kids at the trade deadline and we will be better in a year."

He said, "You don't want to win. You just want the money."

I was getting madder. "Don't give me that shit. I want to win as much as you do, if not more. Because I'm the goddamn coach and what the team does comes back on me."

We had it out, for quite a while, but of course nothing changed. We moved some players at the deadline, but didn't get anyone back who could really improve the team. It was frustrating because it didn't look like the coming year was going to be much better.

It was the phone messages that pissed me off the most: "You couldn't coach a good fucking peewee team." He was hiding behind a phone leaving a damn message, which I thought was very unprofessional—and cowardly, to be quite honest. I told him that, too.

He didn't come into the coaches' office after a game, and he never stuck around to say anything to me. I don't know if that's his style when it comes to confronting people—that maybe he's one of those guys who would rather do it by phone, so he doesn't have to worry about you saying anything back to him. But I didn't hide behind a message. I called him directly and we met face to face. Maybe the result was a pissing match, but it was necessary. He stopped leaving messages in January, and I never heard another word from him after that. Sometimes he would sit in the stands watching practice. I felt like I was back in the Ballard days, with Harold sitting on high in the seats at the Gardens.

As tough as that year was, it was a learning year. It wasn't fun losing. It wasn't easy for the players, either, and we had some good kids—guys who worked their tails off and did the best they could. I couldn't have asked any more from them. They gave all they had, and for their sake I tried to keep things as positive as they could be. We lost 24 in a row to finish the season. I still hold the OHL record for fewest wins in a season, with a grand total of three.

Obviously, with a 3-56-7-2 record we finished dead last, which meant we had the first overall pick in the draft. We took Patrick O'Sullivan, a left winger who was playing with the US National Team Development Program. He was a talented kid, for sure, a helluva player, but he also had some serious issues with his father. Later in life, he talked openly about taking emotional and physical abuse from his father; he even wrote a book about it. So here's a kid already having issues in his life and Mississauga takes him first overall. There were some other really good players available that year: Nathan Horton went number two to Oshawa, Sault Ste. Marie took Jeff Carter third, Mike Richards went fourth to Kitchener, Corey Perry went fifth to London. All had great junior and NHL careers. Patrick did have a terrific first season, leading the team with 34 goals and 92 points, but I wasn't around to coach him.

One Monday morning in May, I got a call from Elliott Kerr. He said, "Don wants you to resign by Friday, or else he's going to fire you." I said, "Okay, let's have a press conference. We'll do it Wednesday. I'll just say I'm moving on to do something else and you just pay me the second year on my contract and everyone's happy." I quickly discovered Don didn't want to pay me. I told Elliott I wasn't resigning, then. He could fire me if he wanted, but I wasn't walking away from a year's pay. Why resign if it means he doesn't have to pay me?

So, Friday came and Don fired me. Actually, he had Elliott fire me. Don probably didn't have the balls to do it in person.

In the end, I wasn't entirely sure who had the ultimate say with the team, although it felt like it was Don. He was instrumental in getting the expansion team and then working with Mississauga mayor Hazel McCallion to get it into the Hershey Centre, as it was called then. I was told Don owned 23.3 percent of the team. Trevor, who was also Don's lawyer, had 13.3 percent. An investment fund had 33.3 percent. Elliott came in late and had a 30 percent share. Whatever the structure, Don had a big say.

Fast-forward to July. Because I had signed late in July the previous summer, Elliott called and said my pay for the second year of the deal was starting in a week. The problem was that Don was only going to pay me for six weeks. I told Elliott, "Tell Don I'll see him in court." He said, "I don't know if you want to do that. He's got more money and he can ride this out." I didn't really give a shit about that. It was the principle. I had signed a two-year contract. He fired me, and as far as I was concerned he had to pay me. I talked to a labour lawyer, who looked at the contract and agreed. I had an option year, too, and the labour lawyer said they should also pick up the option year because of the circumstances.

We went back and forth with Elliott, who I liked and who treated me well, and we got the payment bumped up to ten months. I also got to keep the team cellphone for ten months. I signed off on the settlement. In hindsight, I should have pushed for every dime the team owed me, but at that point, I just wanted to move on.

A few years later, I was watching *Hockey Night in Canada* and Don's "Coach's Corner" segment comes on. That week Bert Templeton, who was coaching in Sudbury, had gotten fired. Don said—I couldn't believe what I was hearing—"Can you believe that [Sudbury] owner doesn't want to pay him?" I wanted to jump through the TV and grab him by the throat. It was exactly what Don had done to me. Bert had to sue the team, and his $400,000 lawsuit for breach of contract was settled out of court.

The next season, with first overall pick O'Sullivan and a couple more draft picks to work with, Don took over as the IceDogs' head coach, with his nephew Steve Cherry as an assistant. Steve was already in place when I came in, which was fine. He was just getting started in coaching, so he didn't have a lot of experience, but I liked him and he worked hard. Joe Washkurak was Don's other assistant. They had a better team than mine, but still finished with an 11-47-6-4 record.

After I left the IceDogs, I applied for twenty, maybe twenty-five jobs every spring and summer—in the ECHL, AHL, junior hockey —but I never got another job coaching pros or juniors. I've always wondered about that. Still do.

That season with Mississauga certainly was, in an odd way, a season to remember—and one to forget. Not to mention a reminder to listen to my instincts. When things don't feel right, pay attention.

16

OUT FROM UNDER THE INFLUENCE

When I first quit drinking, in Charleston, I guess you could say I'd had an epiphany. That was the moment when I said, *Okay, I'm not going to let this get in the way of my job, or my family, or anything else.*

I didn't drink at home back then, or seldom did, because of the boys. I didn't want to drink around them. Joyce didn't like me drinking to the point where I would get a little sloppy. Or very sloppy. Deep down, I didn't either. Joyce never harped on it. She said what she had to say and that was it. I totally understood how she felt, because I would get to a point where I wouldn't be able to talk properly—just sloppy—and it wasn't a good look.

How much of my childhood, my upbringing, was influencing my adult life? I don't know the answer, but I definitely think there was a correlation of some kind. After all, I'd grown up in party central, being around a lot of drinkers, a lot of alcoholics. I loathed it when I was young. I had so many family members who were alcoholics,

I'm convinced it's a genetic thing—and I was predisposed to be an alcoholic. Early on, when I started drinking—seventeen, eighteen years old—it didn't seem like a big deal. But over the years, it got uglier. So once I quit, after that night in Norfolk, and managed to go almost fifteen years without a drink, I thought it was a great accomplishment. I was feeling good. Too good, maybe, because I eventually let my guard down.

When my father-in-law, Dr. Harold Stewart, passed away on September 29, 2008, we went to Charlottetown for the service. Joyce's brother Bobby who played 575 games in the NHL with Boston, California, Cleveland, St. Louis and Pittsburgh, came home. Another brother, Gordie, was there, too. My father-in-law didn't drink much, but he loved a Scotch in the evening. Anyway, there was a bottle of Chivas that Bobby had once brought for him that hadn't been opened. We took it out and raised a few toasts. Even Joyce, who wasn't a drinker, had a little shot. When she saw me have mine, she didn't say so at the time, but she was terrified.

After that, I guess I didn't see the need to refuse myself any longer. And for a while, drinking wasn't a problem. Everything was under control. I would go home, I'd have a beer or two when I was barbecuing, a glass of wine with dinner, and that would be about it. By spring, when my fiftieth birthday rolled around, I was getting used to drinking again. We had a big bash at the house to celebrate, and I drank quite a bit. But exactly two months later, after I got stopped and charged with a DUI, things got much worse. In many ways, my world started to crumble.

Let's go back a few years. After I stopped coaching the IceDogs in 2001, I started doing some television work, first with The Score and then with Leafs TV. I also signed a contract with the Leafs to be an ambassador, because the TV gig alone didn't pay a lot. I did that for about six years—the TV, some public appearances for the Leafs, and any other events that came along—before I stopped the TV work and was doing just appearances.

I had coached in minor hockey a year or so earlier with the Toronto Nationals minor midget team (sixteen-year-olds) and I enjoyed it. I had Jeff Skinner, Tyler Seguin and Jamie Oleksiak, who all went on to the NHL. My old teammate Steve Thomas was coaching the Marlies. His son, Christian, was on that team. I was still doing stuff for the Leafs at the time—appearances, playing alumni games—so I was making pretty good money. The owner of the minor midget team took care of me very well, too. But I only coached for the one year. It was the year my father-in-law died, the year I allowed myself to start drinking again.

On July 14, 2009, everything changed.

That weekend, I had been in Gravenhurst, Ontario, which is about a two-hour drive north of Toronto, with a bunch of NHL alumni for a charity golf tournament. We had played golf on Saturday and stayed up until 4:30 in the morning playing poker. We golfed again on Sunday, a 1 p.m. tee-off. Afterwards, I headed home in my Ford F-150 pickup, along with Dennis Maruk and Billy Derlago. I felt fine to drive.

I drove down Highway 11, then Highway 400, and then jumped onto Highway 407. I got off at Pine Valley Drive and drove a few blocks north to a strip mall where Billy had parked his car. When we got there, I got out of the truck. My hip was bothering me a lot back then, after all those years of poorly tended hip pointers. I'd been driving for a few hours, so I was hanging on to the side of the truck, stretching my hip. Some person in a store thought I was holding on because I couldn't stand up, and they called the police. The caller said I was staggering, and that when I left the plaza I drove over a curb.

I got back on the highway. An officer followed me for about three miles before pulling me over at around 8 p.m. He said he didn't see any erratic driving, but he pulled me over and put me in the cruiser anyway. He didn't do a breathalyzer at the scene, and I didn't take one until about three and a half hours later.

I was charged with impaired driving and driving with over 80 milligrams of alcohol in 100 millilitres of blood. That seemed impossible.

I pleaded not guilty.

After that, there was no work for me at all. Nothing. I had left the Leafs and now the appearances, the banquets, the golf tour-naments—it all stopped. I wasn't employable. No one wanted me, and it's not like I had a couple of business degrees in my back pocket to fall back on. The sudden hard times hit Joyce hard, sent her into a difficult depression that caused her to lose twenty-five pounds. That was the smallest she'd been since we'd met. She was at her limit.

With no money coming in, we were draining every dollar we had saved. Joyce was supply teaching and coaching. We had one kid in university. It's an expensive time of life. Suddenly losing so much of our income wasn't a comfortable feeling, and it got worse. My drinking quickly went from moderate to bad.

It took two years and nine months from the time I was charged until the day I was cleared of charges. That was a wicked thirty-three months. First, I had all the pressure of going through a trial, and of not knowing whether I would be found innocent. Then we had the money problems. The worst part was not being able to do anything about it because, obviously, the charge made headlines. I was a former captain of the Toronto Maple Leafs, living in the Greater Toronto Area. You think there's scrutiny in Toronto when you play a few bad games? Every time we went to court, the proceedings were in the news.

The drinking got to the point where I'd go to the liquor store when it opened in the morning and buy some vodka. Then I'd buy a bottle of Gatorade, pour some of it out and pour the vodka in. I'd keep it in my car, and at night I'd go out to the garage to drink. I wasn't driving. I'd just sit in there while Joyce was in bed.

In the fall of 2011, while the trial was going on, I was asked by the Oakville Rangers if I would coach their minor midget team. Obviously, I didn't have anything going on, and I knew I could make a few bucks doing it, so I said yes. About two months into the season, in November, the mounting pressure of the trial and my worsening drinking problem got the better of me. We were in Whitby, just east of Toronto, for a tournament. I was at a restaurant near the hotel, drinking hard, and the next day I was late getting to our game. For a coach to do that, for the reason it happened—when I'm supposed to be setting a disciplined example for a group of competitive young men? It was a disaster.

Soon after, the owners of the team told me they were going to replace me. It hurt, but I deserved it. I paid back what they'd paid me to coach, which was the right thing to do, because I hadn't been at my best. I knew they were making the right decision for them. It was the right decision for me, too, because it helped me figure out what the hell I had to do—and that was get help.

Joyce was done with me. This was one embarrassment too many. She was reaching out to friends and family, trying to figure out where she could go, when I went to see a doctor. About a month after the coaching debacle, on December 4, I entered GreeneStone Muskoka, a rehab facility a couple of hours north of Toronto. It's the same place Rob Ford, the late mayor of Toronto, visited a few years ago. The NHL Players' Emergency Assistance Fund paid for my stay, and for that I will be forever grateful. I was there for forty-five days in all, with a short break at home for Christmas. Joyce and Jeff came up once for a Sunday visit.

Before I went in, Justin, my younger son, was playing with San Antonio of the AHL, and they were in Rochester for a game. I drove to the game to tell him that I was leaving to get help. I wanted him to hear it from me. I didn't want him finding out from someone else. Just like everyone in the family, he was supportive, happy even that I had decided to man up and get control of this problem. I know Jeff had a hard time with everything, but he was good. And Joyce decided to stick with me.

Being away, seeing and talking with other people who were in the same situation with alcoholism or, in many cases, a lot worse, helped me to realize that I couldn't drink. There was no acceptable limit for me, behind the wheel or anywhere else, because I'd eventually break whatever limits I set. There were only two years in a twenty-five-year period where I was drinking heavily. Both times I quit, the drinking had gotten bad enough to convince me do something about it. This time it needed to be for good.

The rehab centre didn't feel like a prison or anything, but there was a routine and we had to follow it. We had meetings with counsellors, some private meetings, group meetings, some physical activity, and we had to be there for all the meals. If you didn't show up for something and you weren't in your room, there was a chance you could get kicked out. I didn't struggle with the routine, but it was tough being away from home.

The original plan was for me to stay there for thirty days, in part because once I arrived I didn't miss drinking at all. But one day I got mad at a woman who kept interrupting meetings. I got frustrated and spoke up about it. I didn't go crazy; I just spoke my mind. The counsellors said I had an anger-management problem and kept me in for another fifteen days.

Like the first time I quit, I was determined to not let drinking get the better of me again. After I got home from GreeneStone in January, I attended Alcoholics Anonymous and would continue to do so regularly during the year to come. But long before the year was up, the source of the stress that had been driving me to drink so much finally came to a head.

"You are free to go, Mr. Vaive."

I can't put into words the emotions that swept over me when I heard Justice Anne-Marie Hourigan say those words in a New-market courtroom on April 12, 2012. Her decision marked the end of three terrible years, dating back to July 2009, when that charge of driving under the influence turned my life upside down. It had been a frightening and draining experience.

During the court proceedings, I testified that I'd been okay to drive. My lawyer kept asking the officer why it took so long to get the breathalyzer test. Finally, the officer said they'd had to call someone in from a couple of hours away to fix the machine. When I eventually took the test, it read that I was almost two times over the legal limit, which didn't make sense. I hadn't had a beer since the afternoon, and the first test was at 10:40 p.m. I took a second a little after eleven o'clock. Was the machine working properly? The officer insisted that yes, it had been fixed. But finally he had to admit there was a chance it wasn't working properly. Because the breathalyzer reading wasn't taken within two hours of my being stopped, the judge couldn't accept the results.

As I told the court, on the Saturday of that weekend I'd had several drinks over golf, dinner and a late-night poker game. I didn't sleep well that night (yes, it was a short night) because I have sleep apnea and didn't have my machine with me, which was my fault. On Sunday, I had one beer before golf, four light beers during the game, and one at the clubhouse afterwards. I thought I had paced myself over the day.

The officer had testified that my eyes were bloodshot. I hadn't had much sleep over the weekend and was tired. He also said I had a wet stain on my shorts. That was true. I've always had that bladder problem that plagued me as a kid. I keep a big milk jug in my truck in case I can't pull over in time to pee. When I got in the police car and they were taking me to the station, I obviously couldn't go to the bathroom, and I peed my shorts a little bit. That was a big point of contention in court.

The prosecutor kept hammering away at it, like I was trying to fool him or something. But I was just telling the court the way it is. It's the way my body is, and I've been like this since I was a kid. There are times when I have to go, and I know I won't always have time to pull over or get to the next gas station, so I keep that jug in my truck.

There was also a video taken at the police station. The judge said, "The videotape speaks for itself. At no time was he observed to be stumbling or swaying or off balance." She dismissed the charge. I was cleared by the courts, and I was grateful. Just the same, the lesson was clear, and it's one I've embraced. Alcohol and driving don't mix. And I was done with alcohol.

It was still a tough time, though. We had dug deep into our savings—there wasn't a lot left at this point—and it took a few months before I was asked to make any appearances. It was a relief, but it was still slow going. Work didn't really get going until after the holidays, in early 2013. I took a course through the NHL Alumni Association, a speaking course, and it was quite helpful with organizing talking points. I did half a dozen or so speaking engagements. I wasn't exactly comfortable doing it. I would rather have been signing autographs and talking with people a few at a time, but it was good to be earning a living again.

Much of what I talked about was how hockey was similar to business because you had to work as a team to be successful. I'd talk about the simple things like that—teamwork and co-operation, and working hard to work your way up the ladder. And I would tell young people, many in their first or second year in business, to talk to and listen to people who are successful and who have experience. They know a few things, and hearing them out can help you advance your career. That's no different than on a hockey team, or on any other sports team—talk to the veteran guys, the coaches, people who have been there and done that for so long. Ask them questions and learn.

As for my drinking, I haven't had a drink since December 4, 2011. I'm happy I was able to walk away before anything too damaging happened. In the end, my best defence against whatever trouble drinking causes me isn't going to be counting bottles and cans or managing how much I drink in a day before I drive a truck or go home to Joyce—it's simply not drinking. I'll never have to worry about drinking and driving if I just don't drink, and we don't keep liquor in the house anymore. We never give it as a gift, either. Addiction can grab hold of you, and you don't always see it coming. I don't think people always understand that.

I witnessed first-hand what my grandfather went through. He wouldn't drink for a year or two, but as soon as he had one drink he'd be hammered for two straight weeks. My dad had a tough time with alcohol, too. He had a tough life, period. He watched his older brother Richard get run down by a drunk driver when they were very young. Their father worked in construction, and that's how my father got into it at a young age, which led eventually to his terrible accident. Who knows what kind of pain he lived with after that.

Dad drank too much when he got older. When my mom passed away, on January 7, 2010, he basically went into a spiral. We bought him one of those mobile chairs, so he was able to go see his buddies at the bar. I think he just lost his will to live after mom passed away, although he did live another six years. But his quality of life wasn't very good. I don't think he enjoyed life after she passed, but who does, when that happens?

My sister looked after Dad, especially during his last year and a half. He was on oxygen, but he was still smoking. He was stubborn, like me. He died on March 16, 2016, at Cape Breton Hospital. I couldn't go home for the funeral. Or I decided to not go home. I had four or five appearances booked. This wasn't very long after the trial, so the money was important. It's my work, and I couldn't back out of the arrangements. I got shit from everyone in my family because I didn't go home for the funeral. But they all had regular jobs, so they were still getting paid. I needed to make those appearances. It doesn't mean I didn't grieve. Later in the spring, when he was buried, I went home.

Seeing up close what drinking probably did to my father and grandfather helped me in my own battles with alcohol, especially after that night in Norfolk, when I said I wasn't going to let it affect my life, my job and my family.

I'd say life has been getting better and better since I got out of rehab and put that trial behind me. The boys are great, and we have a grandson. And, as you might have guessed, Joyce stayed.

So, yeah, the past nine years and counting have been pretty darn good. I owe that to my family, more than anyone. And you don't know who I am until you know them.

17

LUCKY MAN

Despite the games, the injuries, the travelling, the trades, the moving, the drinking, the trial and all the other stuff life threw at me—home was always the best place I could be. I have Joyce and our sons to thank for that. I got a lot of support from them, especially when I was going through the trial and rehab. They never wavered. It was always, "You are who you are, and we're here for you." Knowing I had their support, I could face the troubles life threw at me the way I wanted to: head on.

I first met Joyce Stewart in grade ten. There were two junior high schools in Charlottetown—Birchwood and Queen Charlotte. She went to Queen Charlotte; I went to Birchwood. So we'd never met before high school. Then we were in the same homeroom. I had a buddy, Allan Weatherby, whose locker was right beside hers. I paid him five bucks to swap lockers so I could be beside her. I've never told her that. I've been waiting for the right time, but I always worried she might think it was weird. I don't know if she really liked me at the start, but she sure grew on me—and I guess eventually I grew on her. The rest, as they say, is history. We've been married thirty-eight years and we dated for six years before that. Quite a run. Best five dollars I've ever spent!

Joyce was a very good basketball and volleyball player, a terrific all-around athlete. She played basketball at Acadia University in Nova Scotia for three years and Brandon in Manitoba for her final year. After her first year at Acadia, she played for the Canadian national junior team.

I shouldn't admit this, but I didn't remember our first date until she reminded me about watching her game and going to the new McDonald's. But I do remember that every time I'd drive her home, we'd sit in the driveway and talk until the outside house lights would blink on and off. That was her parents saying it was time for Joyce to come in. It was hilarious; we'd see the lights blink and it was "see you tomorrow."

Probably a year or so into our going out, I was pretty sure she was the one. Having said that, we did break up a few times along the way—nothing major, just stupid stuff. We were young and going our separate ways for hockey and university. We were kind of long-distance friends for a few years. I spent two years in Sherbrooke, saw her in the summer, went to Birmingham— she wasn't impressed with that scene—and then when I went to Vancouver she went to Brandon. She came out to visit me a couple times, once after she was in the Miss Canada pageant and again over Christmas, and that's when I proposed.

I was traded to Toronto not long after that, and the next season she lived with me there. We got married the following summer, on June 6, 1981. I remember *that* date! We were married in her family church in Charlottetown—Spring Park United Church. She was Protestant, I was Catholic. That didn't go over too well with her mother, at first. She was even more concerned that her daughter, a scholar and an athlete, was young and marrying a hockey player. She wanted Joyce to put her education first.

I'm not so sure my parents really accepted it right away either, not because of the religion but because they always thought, especially after we were married, that whenever I wasn't home in the summer it was Joyce's fault. Even while we were dating, I'd be out with her and in their minds she was taking me away from the family. That wasn't fair at all. I just wanted to be with her and not at party central. And before we had kids, we'd come home for a month, a month and a half in the summer. We'd stay with Joyce's parents; they had more space. Once the kids came along, we'd go home for only a few weeks. I don't think my parents thought too much of that. They blamed Joyce, but I wasn't having any of it.

We had 250 people at the wedding. Bill Derlago was my best man. Billy came down to the island a week before and we played some golf and had some fun, a few parties. The men in the wedding party, including Billy and me, had gotten fitted for tuxedos—light grey with dark lapels; no frilly shirt, just the normal tux shirt. But when the tuxedos showed up, they were smaller than they were supposed to be.

On the wedding day, we got dressed at my parents' house. We were running late, but the church wasn't far away—nothing in Charlottetown was very far away. Anyway, when I got in the car, I ripped the ass out of my pants. Luckily, one of my father's sisters was there, and she was a seamstress. So back in the house I went and she sewed up the pants. She didn't have time to fix them well, just well enough. I remember that at one point during the ceremony we had to kneel to light a candle, and our backs were facing the whole church while we were doing it. I was terrified I was going to rip the ass out of them again. It was probably the most gingerly I've ever kneeled in my life. I did rip them again at the reception, and Billy ripped his, but by then we didn't care. We all had a good chuckle after.

After the wedding, Joyce and I left for our honeymoon in Hawaii courtesy of Harold Ballard, or at least he gave us the tickets to get there. Every Christmas, Harold gave the players and coaches two tickets to anywhere American Airlines flew (I'm sure he didn't pay for it). Hawaii was a bit of a hike from Charlottetown, of course, so we split up the travel, flying to Toronto and spending a few days there, and then flying the rest of the way.

We had bought a house in Don Mills, a suburb in midtown Toronto. Life was good for a while. That first year we were married was the year I scored 54 goals. Then I was made Leafs captain. It was good, except we weren't winning. Home was better. Our first son, Jeff, was born in Toronto at Mount Sinai Hospital in October 1985. Justin was born in Buffalo in July 1989. Both were planned, although Joyce had a miscarriage in between, which was very sad. When I was traded from Chicago to Buffalo on the day after Christmas in 1988, Jeff was three years old and Joyce was three or four months pregnant with Justin.

While we were in Buffalo, Jeff started playing hockey when he was about to turn five, and he played there for a few years before we moved to Charleston in August 1993. Unfortunately, they didn't have very established hockey programs there yet. Jeff was almost eight when we moved to South Carolina, and he was a pretty damn good player. In Buffalo, he had tried out for the seven-year-old Junior Sabres when he was six and made the team. To this day I have regrets about the move when it comes to Jeff. He did continue to improve in Charleston, but not like he would have had we stayed in Buffalo.

When we got to Saint John, he was behind all the other players his age, but I don't think it bothered him too much. A few years later, he played AAA with the Oakville Rangers up to his midget year. He played a year of tier 2 with Streetsville, and then went to university at St. Mary's in Halifax. He wasn't good enough to play for the varsity team—that's pretty good hockey. He majored in English and graduated cum laude, with scholarships the whole way through. He played junior with a team outside Halifax for a year or two and that was it for hockey.

He worked hard all through school, landscaping and retail, then as a rep for Molson and stayed on with them for a while after he graduated. He's an amazing writer, very creative and well spoken. He considered a career in journalism before working his way up through a few different companies, and is now in management with Moosehead Breweries and living in Burlington, Ontario. He's married, and he and Kirsten gave us our first grandchild on August 9, 2019—Hunter Richard Vaive!

When Justin was young—we were still in Charleston—I kept asking him if he wanted to learn how to skate, and he kept saying no. But when he turned five he said he wanted to play hockey. I said to him, "You need to learn how to skate to play hockey," and he said, "No, I just want to play hockey." Okay! We got him all the equipment, got him skating and got him into hockey. The first two games, he never moved. He just stood there and waved to us in the stands. Then, all of a sudden, in the third game the puck came to him, hit his stick, and he kind of pushed it and started moving his feet and went down and scored a goal. After that he was a hockey player.

By the time we got to Saint John, he was becoming a pretty good player; he even played for Team New Brunswick. When we moved to Toronto, he played for the Oakville Rangers with Sam Gagner, who went on to be drafted sixth overall by Edmonton and had a pretty good NHL career. Sam's dad, Dave, was also a very good NHL player, mostly with Minnesota and Dallas. Dave was the assistant coach on the boys' team. The next year, he wanted to be the head coach, which he should have been, but they wouldn't give it to him. The politics of minor hockey! So, he left and took Sam, Justin and Cody Goloubef (now part of the Detroit Red Wings organization) to play for the AAA Toronto Marlies. Dave was an assistant with the Marlies, under the very fine head coach James Naylor, and did a fabulous job of teaching and developing the kids, using skills practices that were ahead of the times.

Justin played with the Marlies for four years, and they won the Ontario championship a couple of times. John Tavares, now the captain of the Maple Leafs, joined that team after the first year, so Justin played with him for three years. Akim Aliu, who was in the news in late November 2019 with allegations that a former minor-pro coach had uttered racial slurs toward him, was on that team. Dave did a great job with their skill development. In their minor midget year, they won the OHL Cup, and Justin got drafted by the Sudbury Wolves.

During the draft, which was done over the phone, Mike Foligno, my former teammate in Buffalo, was coaching Sudbury, and Craig Hartsburg, who I played with in Birmingham, was coaching Sault Ste. Marie. In the third round of the draft, Sudbury had the seventeenth pick and the Soo had the eighteenth. Mike called me and asked what Justin was planning to do. Mike's oldest son, Nick, who is now playing in Columbus, had gone to the US National Team Development Program for a year before he went to Sudbury. I told Mike I was pretty sure Justin was going to go to the US program, but I wasn't sure whether he would stay for both years. Mike said he was still going to draft Justin.

Then Hartsy called and asked me what Justin was planning to do. I told him the same thing. Mike ended up taking Justin. We went up to Sudbury after the draft to visit, but Justin was set on going to the US program. He was a pretty smart kid, and as a sixteen-year-old he already knew he was good but not a future superstar. He'd get more ice time in the US program than in junior, and a better chance to develop. He was six foot four, 180 pounds. When he left the program after two years, he was six foot six, 225 pounds. They had a fabulous off-ice program. It was a well-rounded experience: they went to Alaska, they played overseas, and he became a better player. And he played with some really good players in that program, guys like Kevin Shattenkirk, James van Riemsdyk, Colin Wilson, Ian Cole.

Justin got drafted by the Anaheim Ducks in the fourth round, ninety-second overall, in the 2007 NHL Entry Draft. Brian

Burke was the general manager. Justin went to Miami University (Ohio) and had four great years there. In two of those years they got to the Frozen Four, the US college championship, losing once in the final game. Jeff Blashill, head coach of the Detroit Red Wings, was the assistant coach at Miami in Justin's first year. John Hynes, who coaches the Nashville Predators, was the coach of the seventeen-year-olds' team. The guy who coached Justin at the US program when he was sixteen was Ron Rolston, who later coached the Buffalo Sabres. At Miami, for all four years, his coach was Enrico Blasi, who was originally from Toronto—a really talented guy who had been a guest instructor with the Leafs at their 2009 training camp. So Justin got some great coaching.

There was an incredibly sad moment during that time. Brian Burke's youngest son, Brendan, was the video co-ordinator and student manager for the hockey team, a wonderful young man I'd met several times. Brendan made headlines in November 2009 when he told the hockey team he was gay. It was a very brave and honourable thing to do, and the story eventually made its way to the media. Enrico and the team fully supported Brendan, who played some hockey himself. In speaking out against homophobia in sports, especially pro sports, Brendan's voice was starting to be heard on many levels.

Horribly, Brendan and another young man were killed in a car crash on February 5, 2010. Brian was the general manager of the Leafs at the time. Trevor Whiffen, my agent when I was coaching, was the governor for the OHL London Knights. Brian was with him that night watching a game in London. Trevor knew I was at the school to watch some games and he called me with the news. I couldn't believe what I'd just heard. As a parent, losing a child is one of the worst tragedies you could ever contemplate. I couldn't imagine what Brian and his family were going through.

They wanted me to tell Enrico what had happened. After the first period, I was in the stands down near the bench trying to get Enrico's attention. He looked at me in a funny way, like I was a crazy parent who was going to complain about his kid's ice time or something. I told him we had to talk. We went to his office and I told him and the coaching staff what had happened. It was, obviously, a sad and very difficult day.

Justin wound up getting his degree in sports management at Miami and took some coaching courses. Fortunately, he also took a cooking course in his senior year. Today, he's an incredible cook, almost chef calibre. That skill has really helped him adjust to life on his own as a pro—unlike his father, who'd lit his apartment in Birmingham on fire when he dropped a red-hot frying pan on the carpet. I ate out a lot.

Justin didn't go to the Anaheim camp. Burkie was in Toronto by then, and the Ducks decided not to sign Justin when he came out of college. Dale Tallon, who was general manager of the Florida Panthers at the time, and a guy I knew well from Chicago, met with Justin and me. He wound up signing him to an AHL/ECHL contract and invited him to Florida's training camp. We were thrilled. Justin started the season with their Cincinnati affiliate in the ECHL and was called up to San Antonio in the AHL halfway through the season. He had a few more stops in the minors, and then landed again in Cincinnati, where he was a playing assistant coach in 2019–20 before the COVID-19 pandemic shut down the season. I see him coaching full-time when he stops playing.

As I said, I'm a very lucky man on so many levels. Sadly, I saw what happened to my good friend, teammate and roommate Greg Terrion. You never know, that could have been me. And I tried to help Greg. Very sad. I also probably had a minimum of twenty concussions during my career. Four times I was knocked out for sure. Thankfully, so far I have been fine. I had my share of other injuries, too, but the old body is holding up pretty well. I'm still able to play a ton of alumni games, which I enjoy, and I golf every chance I can.

But I am an especially lucky man when it comes to family. I am very proud and I am truly blessed. *I love you*—three words that mean so much to me, mostly because they're true.

18

BY THE NUMBERS

There's a story that has made the rounds. I've heard about it and read it online, but I honestly don't remember it happening.

As the story goes, a fourteen-year-old Brendan Shanahan was skating at a twin rink in Etobicoke, a suburb of Toronto, one August day in 1983, and I was apparently skating on the other rink with some NHLers.

Brendan was quoted in the Newark *Star-Ledger* as saying: "Rick Vaive happened to be skating at an adjoining rink and we were actually in dressing rooms that were right next to each other, I went in when he was sort of settled and asked him for an autograph. I didn't get the best response from Rick Vaive at the time."

I don't remember him asking, and I certainly don't remember saying no to a kid looking for an autograph. But whatever happened, Shanny sure didn't forget it.

The kid from Mimico, which was not far from that rink, became a great player. He was drafted second overall in 1987 by the New Jersey Devils and ultimately was inducted into the Hockey

Hall of Fame. These days, he is president of the Maple Leafs. Anyway, as the story goes, a few years later the Devils were playing in Buffalo and there's Shanny, still remembering that summer day. And he let me know what he thought of it.

"Fast forward four years later and Rick Vaive is waiting for a meaningless faceoff in Buffalo," Shanahan was quoted as saying. "He's now playing for the Sabres. He's lined up next to some 18-year-old kid from New Jersey. When the puck dropped, I attacked Rick Vaive... he couldn't believe the rage I had, not only in attacking him, but it took two (linesmen) to restrain me afterwards and throw me in the penalty box."

The attack was all about the autograph snub.

It's true that some of the Leafs used to skate in Etobicoke in August and early September before training camp. But I don't recall turning down an autograph request. If it did happen that way, it shouldn't have. I should have signed. After games at the Gardens, we'd leave through the Wood Street doors and sign autographs for an hour. It was part of the job, and it was especially fun to see the kids light up. I don't remember having that fight, either.

The funny thing is, Joyce was at the game in Buffalo when Shanny jumped me, and she remembers it as well as Brendan does. Many years later, at a Leafs alumni gathering, Joyce and I got talking to him, a really nice conversation—I had no idea he and I had this history—and Joyce asks why on earth he went after me all those years ago. Poor Shanny. He spent fifteen minutes very graciously explaining himself—it was thirty years ago! The autograph, it turns out, was for someone else.

I like Brendan. He was a great player, obviously—a three-time Stanley Cup champion—and I like what he has done since becoming president of the Maple Leafs in 2014. He has helped to turn the team's fortunes around and make them a contender. And the thing he did that I like the most was deciding to finally retire player numbers. For years, the Leafs would honour players and their numbers, but not retire them. It irked a lot of players; namely the greatest Leaf of all time, Dave Keon. But on October 15, 2016, Brendan put an end to that frustration.

Honouring numbers was something different than probably any organization in pro sports was doing. As a player, I didn't think much about it. If your number was honoured, that was pretty cool. But it was different—most organizations retire numbers. I figured, honoured or retired, it was still up there in the rafters. People saw the banners every time they came into the building. But as time went on and I grew older, I realized the difference, and the importance of retiring numbers.

I think the commitment by the team to make sure no one ever wears your number again gives a little bit more meaning to it all. A great example is 27: Frank Mahovlich and Darryl Sittler, two great players. When Miro Ihnačák came over from Czechoslovakia back in the eighties, they gave him number 27. Here's a guy who had a cup of coffee in the NHL, wasn't a big draft pick, and he's wearing the number of two of the greatest players in Leafs history. That's not right. That's when I started thinking that retiring numbers was better than honouring them. Think about Dave Keon: no one should wear 14. You had James van Riemsdyk, who was a good player, wearing 21, Börje Salming's number. No knock on JVR or anyone else, but it's not right.

I think retiring the numbers was a great decision. One of the reasons Keon didn't come back for alumni functions for many years was because of the honoured numbers. There were other reasons, but once they decided to retire the numbers on opening night 2016—the start of the Leafs 100th anniversary season, so perfect timing—there he was. That was great to see.

And all the guys (or their families, if they had passed away) were told about it by Brendan only just before the ceremony. What an emotional night that was. A total of nineteen players had their numbers retired. Two—Ace Bailey's number 6 and Bill Barilko's number 5—had already been retired, Bailey's because he had his career cut short by injury and Barilko after he perished in a plane crash after scoring the Cup-winning goal in 1951. The others were number 1—Turk Broda and Johnny Bower; number 4—Hap Day and Red Kelly; number 7—King Clancy and Tim Horton; number 9—Ted Kennedy and Charlie Conacher; number 10—Syl Apps and George Armstrong; number 13—Mats Sundin; number 14, a new banner for Keon; number 17—Wendel Clark; number 21—Börje Salming; number 27—Mahovlich and Sittler; and number 93—Doug Gilmour.

It was the right thing to do and wonderfully done.

I won't lie. I hope my number 22 will one day join them, and that it will happen before I'm too old to really enjoy it. To have my family there—it would be fantastic, an incredible honour. But, you know, it was an honour to play for the Toronto Maple Leafs, just to be part of the franchise's history. It's an honour now to be associated with the Leafs alumni, to put on my old colours and skate with so many friends in front of fans, young and old. And it was an honour then, too, to wear a Maple Leafs sweater and number 22.

ACKNOWLEDGEMENTS

Rick: There are so many people I would like to thank. I mentioned my grandmother and Uncle Frank in the dedication, as well as my wife, Joyce, and sons, Jeff and Justin. I also want to thank my parents, who have both passed, for all they sacrificed for me, my sister, Barbara, and my brothers, Steve and Ron. And thanks for all your support over the years.

Thanks to the minor hockey organizations that impacted my career, along with my junior team in Sherbrooke and Birmingham of the WHA. Thanks, also, to the four NHL organizations I played with—Vancouver, Toronto, Chicago and Buffalo—all the owners, coaches, management and teammates. I played with so many great players who were also great people, and many became great friends. I also want to thank the ownership and players during my time coaching in Charleston and Saint John. As for my other coaching stop, in Mississauga, there were a lot of great kids and other people with that team.

I mention it in the book, but eternal gratitude to the NHL Players' Emergency Assistance Fund, which paid for the help I so desperately needed, and to the NHL and Leafs Alumni Associations.

I want to send my best thoughts to three former teammates who are battling hard. I played with Steve Ludzik in Chicago and Buffalo. We were good friends and continue to be good friends to this day. Steve is suffering from Parkinson's disease and is also in need of a liver transplant. Several years ago, I started helping Steve with his golf tournament and celebrity roast to raise money for the Steve Ludzik Foundation, which created the Steve Ludzik Centre for Parkinson's Rehab in St. Catharines, near to where we both now live.

Davey Gorman was a teammate in Birmingham. He was a fourth-round pick of the Montreal Canadiens in 1975. He lives in the Niagara Region as well. One day, a few years ago, Davey woke up and was having trouble talking and walking. Doctors determined he has a form of amyotrophic lateral sclerosis, also known as ALS and Lou Gehrig's disease. He has been working hard in therapy and shares the same doctor and same horrible disease as Mark Kirton, who I played with briefly in Toronto but have known for years. Mark continues to work in the real estate business. Talk about three really tough guys, three of so many good people I was lucky to meet along the way.

Scott: The poet and novelist Ben Okri once wrote, "The fact of storytelling hints at a fundamental human unease, hints at human imperfection. Where there is perfection there is no story to tell."

I think Rick Vaive would agree.

Rick, as you have read, was a great hockey player who probably could have been even greater. If only ... But then, can't we all be a little bit better in our lives and professions? What many didn't know, however, was the story behind Rick's story, the battles he had with drinking and anxiety and life itself.

Over the years, Rick and I had talked about writing a book together, about telling his story. I had covered Rick during most of his time with the Maple Leafs, so I knew a bit of his story, the hockey story. But I didn't know the rest. For many years, for many reasons, I suppose, the book didn't happen until now. Part of it, I'm sure, is that Rick had to be ready to admit there was imperfection in his world and thus a story to tell.

I want to thank Rick for having the courage and determination to follow through with the book project and for telling his compelling story. I'm sure at times it wasn't easy, but it was always easy dealing with him. I also want to thank his wife, Joyce, who is an amazing person herself—a former athlete, Miss Prince Edward Island, and the glue of the Vaive household—for supporting the book and for filling in so many memories and details. Thanks, also, to sons Jeff and Justin.

I also want to express gratitude to Rick's sister, Barbara O'Neill. It wasn't easy for Barb to read about Rick's difficult experiences growing up, but she was of great assistance just the same, always quick to answer the phone or a text.

When we were contemplating who to ask to write the foreword, a few names came up, but one immediately seemed like the best— Bill Watters, who was Rick's agent from the start of his career and has been a friend of mine for many, many years. Bill and his wife, Naddy, were a tremendous influence in Rick's life on and off the ice. Heck, they've been a huge influence in my life.

There are so many others deserving of thanks for their research and sharing of stories to help pull this book together: my journalist friends and former colleagues Lance Hornby, Terry Koshan and Tim Wharnsby, hockey historians Paul Patskou and Kevin Shea, and the Ultimate Leaf Fan and friend of Rick's and mine, Mike Wilson. Kevin's *Toronto Maple Leafs Hockey Club: Official Centennial Publication* (written with Jason Wilson) was a big help in navigating Rick's Toronto years.

There are a lot of former teammates Rick spoke with at alumni events to kick-start his memory, and many I spoke with as well—including Gord and Bob Stellick, who had a front-row seat for the madness that was the Leafs back in the day. Billy Derlago, who was described as being Butch to Rick's Sundance Kid, was also a great help, along with Wendel Clark and Darryl Sittler. There were a few who shared stories off the record but were happy to help.

I want to extend a very special thanks to Craig Pyette, who is a senior editor with Random House Canada. This is the second book I have worked on with Craig, who is a great pro and an absolute pleasure with whom to work. He is patient beyond belief, a steady, guiding and calming hand and really good at what he does. The comfort level in working with Craig is amazing. One of these days we may do a book together that has a little more runway time-wise! A special thanks, as well, to copy editor Linda Pruessen, with whom I worked several years ago, on my book *Hockey Night in Canada—By the Numbers*. Linda is the ultimate pro and an amazingly thorough copy editor. And thanks to the publisher, Anne Collins, without whom this doesn't happen.

I'm sure I have forgotten someone who helped along the way. Sorry, but a blanket thank you.

Finally, a shout-out to my son, Mark, who was locked in the house with a dad who at times was a little prickly as deadlines approached and a virus was turning our world, like yours, upside down.

INDEX

W

Y

Z

Photo courtesy of author

SCOTT MORRISON has provided cogent and colourful hockey analysis since his start in 1979, covering the Maple Leafs and NHL for the *Toronto Sun*. Having reported and provided analysis for Sportsnet and CBC *Hockey Night in Canada*, while making regular appearances across the sports-radio dial, he twice served as president of the Professional Hockey Writers' Association. He has written numerous books, including *100 Years, 100 Moments*. In 2006, he received the Hockey Hall of Fame's Elmer Ferguson Memorial Award. He lives in Toronto with his son, Mark.

Follow @smorrisonmedia on Twitter

Photo courtesy of author

RICK VAIVE played in the NHL from 1979 to 1992, for the Vancouver Canucks, Toronto Maple Leafs, Chicago Blackhawks and Buffalo Sabres. As captain of the Maple Leafs from 1982 to 1986, he set and still holds the franchise record for goals scored in a single season. He coached seven seasons in the minor professional leagues, including an ECHL championship, and one season in the Ontario Hockey League. He makes regular appearances for the Toronto Maple Leafs and NHL alumni.

Follow @rickvaive22 on Twitter

CATCH
22